DISCOVERING BIBLICAL TREASURES

UNDERSTANDING AMOS

A COMMENTARY ON THE BOOK OF AMOS USING ANCIENT BIBLE STUDY
METHODS - UPDATED

Michael Harvey Koplitz

Published by Michael H. Koplitz

Acknowledgments

This work could not have been accomplished without Dr. Anne Davis, who taught me Ancient Bible (Hebraic) study methods, and my two study partners, Rev. Dr. Robert Cook and Pastor Sandra Koplitz. We know that the journey has just started and will last a lifetime. The discovery of the depths of God's Word is waiting for us to find.

Acknowledgments

Table of Contents

Introduction

While I was attending Seminary earning my M. Div. degree, I questioned what the instructors and reference books were saying about the Scriptures. One idea being offered then was that the Bible was full of errors and not factual. I found that attitude disturbing for seminary instructors to be teaching. After all, the Seminary experience is to train pastors to go out into God's world and preach the Bible. How can you preach the Bible if you believe what these instructors are teaching? The methods that were being taught to examine the Bible just seemed inaccurate to me.

After graduating from Seminary, I spent a lot of time reading different views about the Bible. I eventually read the Zohar. This collection of midrash is considered the secret work of the Torah, according to Kabbalists. In addition, I read quite a bit about Messianic Judaism. Their view of the Bible is quite different from the Seminary view.

I decided that the biblical interpretation that was being taught in Seminary was not the biblical interpretation the people heard when Jesus Christ (whose Hebraic name is Yeshua) preached. I went on a quest to learn what the people of Yeshua's day thought about Scripture, and what they thought when the Scriptures were read. This quest led me to Dr. Anne Davis and The Bible Learning University. Dr. Davis was in search of the same thing I was searching. She had made many discoveries that helped me in my quest. I earned the Ph.D. degree from The Bible Learning University in Hebraic Studies in Christianity concentrating on ancient Bible Studies methods.

Finally, I found someone who believed that the church has placed almost 1900 years of their theological ideas about the Scriptures and in many places possibly distorting its original meaning. What is also important to hear is that the basic tenants of Yeshua as God's Messiah, my Lord and Savior, are in the Bible. My faith in Yeshua is stronger now that I have learned from Dr. Davis how to study the Scriptures in the same manner that the people did in Yeshua's day.

I have included an article that describes the differences between Greek learning methods and Hebraic learning methods. Please do not skip this chapter unless you are familiar with ancient Bible study methods because if you do then the analysis and commentary that follows may become difficult for you to understand.

Our God is vast and infinite and so is His Word. May God bless you in your discovery of what God's Word is about.

Amos lived in the 8th century BCE when Uzziah was king of Judah (Southern Kingdom) and Jeroboam II was the King of Israel (Northern Kingdom). He was a contemporary of Hosea. Amos was a simple man who did not have a formal education. He worked as a herdsman and a gatherer of wild figs. He never claimed to have the mantle of a prophet nor the calling of a prophet.

Amos' prophesies were against the enemies of Israel who were Syria, Edom, Philistia, Moab, Ammon and Tyre. These nations would drink from the cup of the fury of the LORD. He then prophesied against Israel because they had engaged in the Baal cult and worship, thus abandoning the LORD.

Amos offers hope to the people by prophesying that a remnant of Israel would survive the wrath of the LORD.[1]

---

[1] Errico, Rocco A., and George M. Lamsa. "Amos." In *Aramaic Light on Ezekiel, Daniel, and the Minor Prophets: A Commentary Based on the Aramaic Language and Ancient Near Eastern Customs*. Smyma, GA: Noohra Foundation, 2012.

The main differences between the Greek method and Hebraic method of teaching

Once you are aware of the two teaching styles, you will determine if you are in a class or reading a book, whether the analysis and/or teaching method is in a Greek or Hebraic method. In the Greek method, the instructor is right because of advanced knowledge. In the college situation, it is because the professor has his/her Ph.D. in some area of study, so one assumes that he or she knows everything about the topic. For example, Rodney Dangerfield played the role of a middle-aged man going to college. His English midterm was to write about Kurt Vonnegut Jr. Since he did not understand any of Vonnegut's books, he hired Vonnegut himself to the write the midterm. When it was returned to him, the English Professor told Dangerfield that whoever wrote the paper knew nothing about Vonnegut. This is an example of the Greek method of teaching. Did the Ph.D. English professor think she knew more about Vonnegut's writings than Vonnegut did?[2]

In the Greek teaching method, the professor or the instructor claims to be the authority. If you are attending a Bible study class and the class leader says, "I will teach you the only way to understand this biblical book," consider the implications. This method is common since most seminaries and Bible colleges teach a Greek method of learning, which is the same method the church has been using for centuries.

Hebraic teaching methods are different. The teacher wants the students to challenge what they hear. It is through questioning that a student can learn. In addition, the teacher wants his/her students to excel to a point where the student becomes the teacher.

It is said that if two rabbis come together to discuss a passage of Scripture, the result will be at least ten different opinions. All points of view are acceptable if biblical evidence can support the points. It is permissible and encouraged for students to have multiple opinions. There is a depth to God's Word, and God wants us to find all His messages that are placed in the Scriptures.

Seeking the meaning of the Scriptures beyond the literal meaning is essential to fully understanding God's Word.[3] The Greek method of learning the Scriptures has prevailed over the centuries. One problem is that only the literal interpretation of Scripture was often viewed as valid, as prompted by Martin Luther's "sola literalis" meaning that only the literal interpretation of Scripture was valid. The Fundamentalist movements

---

[2] *Back to School*. Performed by Rodney Dangerfield. Hollywood: CA: Paper Clip Productions, 1986. DVD.

[3] Davis, Anne Kimball. *The Synoptic Gospels*. MP3. Albuquerque: NM: BibleInteract, 2012.

of today are based on the literal interpretation of the Scripture. Therefore, they do not believe that God placed any deeper, hidden, or secret meanings in the Word.

The students of the Scriptures who learn through Hebraic training and understanding have drawn a different conclusion. The Hebrew language itself leads to different interpretations because of the construction of the language. The Hebraic method of Bible study opens avenues of thought about God's revelations in the Scripture that may have never been considered. A question may be raised about the Scripture being studied for which there may not be an immediate answer. If so, it becomes the responsibility of the learners to uncover the meaning. Also, remember that multiple opinions about the meaning of Scripture are also acceptable if they can be supported by Scripture.

Methodology

The method employed is to use First Century Scripture study methods integrated with the customs and culture of Yeshua's day to examine the Hebrew and Christian Scriptures, thus gathering a deeper understanding by learning the Scriptures in the way the people of Yeshua's day did.

In typical Rabbinic tradition, I had two study partners. Each one served a different function by looking at the research as I put it together. Rev. Dr. Robert Cook, D. Min., an ordained Elder in the United Methodist Church, has been a study partner in different areas of theology and church leadership. He became interested in Hebraic studies when I started sharing Zohar and Midrash with him. He also completed the entire Disciple program as a student and teacher. My second study partner is my wife, Sandra Koplitz, MS. Sandy and I took the instruction class on teaching the Disciple Bible study program and she takes part in the Zohar study group. Sandy is a licensed local pastor in the United Methodist Church.

The Process of Discovery

I have titled the method of analyzing a passage of Scripture in a Hebraic manner the "Process of Discovery." This method was developed by the author, bringing together the various areas of linguistic and cultural understanding. There are several sections to the process, and not all the sections apply to every passage of Scripture. The overall result of developing this process is to give the reader a framework into the ideas being presented.

The "Process of Discovery" starts with a Scripture passage. If the passage is in a poetic form, it is identified. Possible poetic techniques include parallelism, chiastic structures, and repetition. Formatting the passage in its poetic form allows the reader to visualize what the first century CE listener was hearing. The chiasms are labeled by their corresponding sections, for example: A, B, C, B', A'. Not all passages of the Scriptures have a poetic form.

The next step is to "question the narrative," which is accomplished by assuming the reader knows nothing about the passage. Therefore, the questions go from the simple to the complex. The next task is to identify any linguistic patterns. Linguistic patterns include, but are not limited to: irony, simile, metaphor, symbolism, idioms, hyperbole, figurative language, personification, and allegory.

Any translation inconsistencies discovered between the English NASB version and either the Hebrew or Greek versions are identified. Sometimes a Hebrew or Greek word can be translated in more than one way. Inconsistencies also can be created by the translation committee, which may have used traditional language instead of the actual translation. The decision of the translation committee can be found in the Preface or Introduction to the Bible. Perhaps some inconsistencies were intentionally added to convey some deeper meaning, therefore, the inconsistencies need to be examined.

Echoes of the Hebrew Scriptures in the Christian Scripture are identified. This occurs when a passage from the Hebrew Scripture is used in the Christian Scripture or when a Mitzvot is directly discussed in the Christian Scriptures.[4] In addition, echoes can be found when Torah (Genesis through Deuteronomy) passages are used in other Hebrew Bible books. Besides echoes, cross-references are listed. A cross reference is a reference to another verse in the Scripture which can assist the reader to understand the verse that is being read.

The names of persons mentioned in the passage are listed. Many of the Hebrew names have meaning and may be associated with places or actions. Jewish parents used to name their children based on what they felt God had in store for their child. An example of this is Abraham, whose original name was Abram, and was changed to mean eternal father (in this case Abram's name was changed by God to Abraham, showing a function he was to perform). When the Hebrew Bible gives names, many of the occurrences will show something special to the reader/listener. The same importance can hold true for the names of places. The time to travel between places can supply insight to the event.

Keywords are identified in a verse when they are important to an understanding of that passage. There are no rules for selecting the keywords. Searching for other occurrences of the keywords in Scripture in a concordance is necessary to understand how the word was being used; this must be done in either Hebrew or Greek, not in English. A classic Hebraic approach is to find the usage of a word in the Scripture by finding other verses that contain the word. The usage of a word, in its original language, is discovered by searching the Scripture in the word's language. The verses that contain the word being researched are identified and a pattern for the usage of the word is discerned. Each verse is examined to see what the usage of the word is which, may reveal a pattern for the word's usage. For Hebrew words, the first usage of the word in the Scripture, especially if used in the Torah, is important. For the Greek words, the Christian Scriptures are used

---

[4] Mitzvot are the 613 commandments found in the Torah that please God. There are positive and negative commandments. The list was first development by Maimonides. The full list can be found at: ttp://www.jewfaq.org/613.htm.

to determining the word usage in the Scripture. Sometimes finding the equivalent Greek word in the Septuagint and then analyzing its usage in Hebrew can be very helpful.

The Rules of Hillel for Bible understanding can be used when applicable. Hillel was a Torah scholar who lived shortly before Yeshua's day. Hillel developed several rules for Torah students to interpret the Scriptures which are referred to as halachic midrash. In several cases, these rules are helpful in the analysis of the Scripture.

After the linguistic analysis is complete, an examination of the cultural implications will be examined. The culture is important because it is not specifically referenced in the biblical narratives as shown earlier.

From the linguistic analysis and the cultural understanding, it is possible to get a deeper meaning of the Scripture beyond the literal meaning of the plaintext. That is what the listeners of Yeshua's time were doing. They put the linguistics and the culture together without even having to contemplate it. They did it.

This will lead to a conclusion or a set of conclusions about what the passage is discussing. Most of the time, the Hebraic analysis leads to the desire for a deeper analysis to fully understand what Yeshua was discussing or what was happening to Him. Whatever the result, a new deeper understanding of the Scripture will be obtained.

The components of the Process of Discovery are:

    Linguistics Section

        Linguistic Structure of the Scripture

        Discussion

        Questioning the Passage

        Verse Comparison on citations or proof text

        Translation inconsistencies

        People's names

        Name of places

        Word Study

        Scripture cross references

        Echoes

        Rules of Hillel

        Main/Center Point

Culture Section

Discussion

Questioning the passage culturally

Culture and Linguistics Section

Discussion

Only the sections that apply to each chapter are presented.

Amos Chapter One

Language

New American Standard 1995	Hebrew
[1] The words of Amos, who was among the sheepherders from Tekoa, which he envisioned in visions concerning Israel in the days of Uzziah king of Judah, and in the days of Jeroboam son of Joash, king of Israel, two years before the earthquake. [2] He said, "The LORD roars from Zion And from Jerusalem He utters His voice; And the shepherds' pasture grounds mourn, And the summit of Carmel dries up." [3] Thus says the LORD, "For three transgressions of Damascus and for four I will not revoke its *punishment*, Because they threshed Gilead with *implements* of sharp iron. [4] "So I will send fire upon the house of Hazael And it will consume the citadels of Ben-hadad. [5] "I will also break the *gate* bar of Damascus, And cut off the inhabitant from the valley of Aven, And him who holds the scepter, from Beth-eden; So the people of Aram will go exiled to Kir," Says the LORD. [6] Thus says the LORD, "For three transgressions of Gaza and for four I will not revoke its *punishment*, Because they deported an entire population To deliver *it* up to Edom. [7] "So I will send fire upon the wall of Gaza And it will consume her citadels. [8] "I will also cut off the inhabitant from Ashdod, And him who holds the scepter, from Ashkelon; I will even unleash My power upon Ekron, And the remnant of the Philistines will perish," Says the Lord GOD. [9] Thus says the LORD, "For three transgressions of Tyre and for four I will not revoke its *punishment*, Because they delivered up an entire population to Edom And did not remember *the* covenant of brotherhood.	1 דִּבְרֵי עָמוֹס אֲשֶׁר־הָיָה בַנֹּקְדִים מִתְּקוֹעַ אֲשֶׁר חָזָה עַל־יִשְׂרָאֵל בִּימֵי עֻזִּיָּה מֶלֶךְ־יְהוּדָה וּבִימֵי יָרָבְעָם בֶּן־יוֹאָשׁ מֶלֶךְ יִשְׂרָאֵל שְׁנָתַיִם לִפְנֵי הָרָעַשׁ: 2 וַיֹּאמַר יְהוָה מִצִּיּוֹן יִשְׁאָג וּמִירוּשָׁלַ͏ִם יִתֵּן קוֹלוֹ וְאָבְלוּ נְאוֹת הָרֹעִים וְיָבֵשׁ רֹאשׁ הַכַּרְמֶל: פ 3 כֹּה אָמַר יְהוָה עַל־שְׁלֹשָׁה פִּשְׁעֵי דַמֶּשֶׂק וְעַל־אַרְבָּעָה לֹא אֲשִׁיבֶנּוּ עַל־דּוּשָׁם בַּחֲרֻצוֹת הַבַּרְזֶל אֶת־הַגִּלְעָד: 4 וְשִׁלַּחְתִּי אֵשׁ בְּבֵית חֲזָאֵל וְאָכְלָה אַרְמְנוֹת בֶּן־הֲדָד: 5 וְשָׁבַרְתִּי בְּרִיחַ דַּמֶּשֶׂק וְהִכְרַתִּי יוֹשֵׁב מִבִּקְעַת־אָוֶן וְתוֹמֵךְ שֵׁבֶט מִבֵּית עֶדֶן וְגָלוּ עַם־אֲרָם קִירָה אָמַר יְהוָה: פ 6 כֹּה אָמַר יְהוָה עַל־שְׁלֹשָׁה פִּשְׁעֵי עַזָּה וְעַל־אַרְבָּעָה לֹא אֲשִׁיבֶנּוּ עַל־הַגְלוֹתָם גָּלוּת שְׁלֵמָה לְהַסְגִּיר לֶאֱדוֹם: 7 וְשִׁלַּחְתִּי אֵשׁ בְּחוֹמַת עַזָּה וְאָכְלָה אַרְמְנֹתֶיהָ: 8 וְהִכְרַתִּי יוֹשֵׁב מֵאַשְׁדּוֹד וְתוֹמֵךְ שֵׁבֶט מֵאַשְׁקְלוֹן וַהֲשִׁיבוֹתִי יָדִי עַל־עֶקְרוֹן וְאָבְדוּ שְׁאֵרִית פְּלִשְׁתִּים אָמַר אֲדֹנָי יְהוָה: פ 9 כֹּה אָמַר יְהוָה עַל־שְׁלֹשָׁה פִּשְׁעֵי־צֹר וְעַל־אַרְבָּעָה לֹא אֲשִׁיבֶנּוּ עַל־הַסְגִּירָם גָּלוּת שְׁלֵמָה לֶאֱדוֹם וְלֹא זָכְרוּ בְּרִית אַחִים: 10 וְשִׁלַּחְתִּי אֵשׁ בְּחוֹמַת צֹר וְאָכְלָה אַרְמְנֹתֶיהָ: פ 11 כֹּה אָמַר יְהוָה עַל־שְׁלֹשָׁה פִּשְׁעֵי אֱדוֹם וְעַל־אַרְבָּעָה לֹא אֲשִׁיבֶנּוּ עַל־רָדְפוֹ בַחֶרֶב אָחִיו וְשִׁחֵת רַחֲמָיו וַיִּטְרֹף לָעַד אַפּוֹ וְעֶבְרָתוֹ שְׁמָרָה נֶצַח: 12 וְשִׁלַּחְתִּי אֵשׁ בְּתֵימָן וְאָכְלָה אַרְמְנוֹת בָּצְרָה: פ 13 כֹּה אָמַר יְהוָה עַל־שְׁלֹשָׁה פִּשְׁעֵי בְנֵי־עַמּוֹן וְעַל־אַרְבָּעָה לֹא אֲשִׁיבֶנּוּ עַל־בִּקְעָם הָרוֹת הַגִּלְעָד לְמַעַן הַרְחִיב אֶת־גְּבוּלָם: 14 וְהִצַּתִּי אֵשׁ בְּחוֹמַת רַבָּה וְאָכְלָה אַרְמְנוֹתֶיהָ בִּתְרוּעָה בְּיוֹם מִלְחָמָה בְּסַעַר בְּיוֹם סוּפָה: 15 וְהָלַךְ מַלְכָּם בַּגּוֹלָה הוּא וְשָׂרָיו יַחְדָּו אָמַר יְהוָה: פ

[10] "So I will send fire upon the wall of Tyre And it will consume her citadels."

[11] Thus says the LORD, "For three transgressions of Edom and for four I will not revoke its *punishment*, Because he pursued his brother with the sword, While he stifled his compassion; His anger also tore continually, And he maintained his fury forever.

[12] "So I will send fire upon Teman And it will consume the citadels of Bozrah."

[13] Thus says the LORD, "For three transgressions of the sons of Ammon and for four I will not revoke its *punishment*, Because they ripped open the pregnant women of Gilead In order to enlarge their borders.

[14] "So I will kindle a fire on the wall of Rabbah And it will consume her citadels Amid war cries on the day of battle, And a storm on the day of tempest.

[15] "Their king will go into exile, He and his princes together," says the LORD.

Process of Discovery

Linguistics Section

Linguistic Structure

[Introduction] [1] The words of Amos, who was among the sheepherders from Tekoa, which he envisioned in visions concerning Israel in the days of Uzziah king of Judah, and in the days of Jeroboam son of Joash, king of Israel, two years before the earthquake. [2] He said, "The LORD roars from Zion And from Jerusalem He utters His voice; And the shepherds' pasture grounds mourn, And the summit of Carmel dries up."

[Damascus] [3] Thus says the LORD, "For three transgressions of Damascus and for four I will not revoke its *punishment*, Because they threshed Gilead with *implements* of sharp iron. [4] "So I will send fire upon the house of Hazael And it will consume the citadels of Ben-hadad. [5] "I will also break the *gate bar* of Damascus, And cut off the inhabitant from the valley of Aven, And him who holds the scepter, from Beth-eden; So the people of Aram will go exiled to Kir," Says the LORD.

[Gaza] [6] Thus says the LORD, "For three transgressions of Gaza and for four I will not revoke its *punishment*, Because they deported an entire population To deliver *it* up to Edom. [7] "So I will send fire upon the wall of Gaza And it will consume her citadels. [8] "I will also cut off the inhabitant from Ashdod, And him who holds the scepter, from Ashkelon; I will even unleash My power upon Ekron, And the remnant of the Philistines will perish," Says the Lord GOD.

[Tyre] [9] Thus says the LORD, "For three transgressions of Tyre and for four I will not revoke its *punishment*, Because they delivered up an entire population to Edom And did not remember *the* covenant of brotherhood. [10] "So I will send fire upon the wall of Tyre And it will consume her citadels."

[Edom] [11] Thus says the LORD, "For three transgressions of Edom and for four I will not revoke its *punishment*, Because he pursued his brother with the sword, While he stifled his compassion; His anger also tore continually, And he maintained his fury forever. [12] "So I will send fire upon Teman And it will consume the citadels of Bozrah."

[Ammon] [13] Thus says the LORD, "For three transgressions of the sons of Ammon and for four I will not revoke its *punishment*, Because they ripped open the pregnant women of Gilead In order to enlarge their borders. [14] "So I will kindle a fire on the wall of Rabbah And it will consume her citadels Amid war cries on the day of battle, And a storm on the day of tempest. [15] "Their king will go into exile, He and his princes together," says the LORD.

Discussion

The first chapter of Amos commences with Amos' announcement of who he was and when he had his visions. It should be noted that Amos does not say that his visions were from the LORD. However, he responds to the visions as if the LORD did give them to him. The date of Amos' prophecies are also given.

Questioning the Passage

1. What does the phrase "For three transgressions of Damascus and for four I will not revoke its punishment (Amos 1:3 NAU)" mean?

    This phrase is repeated for the offenses of the nations in the prophecy. It means that the LORD will tolerate the three cardinal sins of idolatry, murder and adultery. The fourth cardinal sin is the persecution of the Jewish nation.[5] The LORD's justice was invoked by the fourth cardinal sin.

2. Where was the town of Tekoa located? (v. 1)

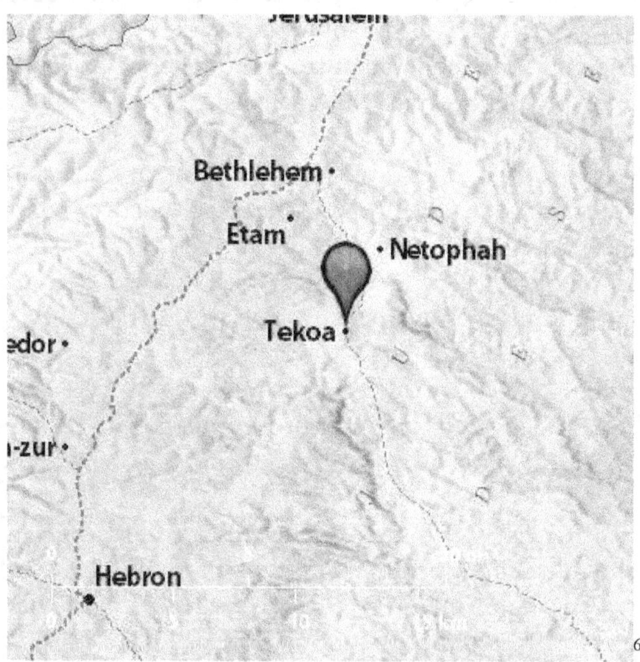

[6]

3. What is the date of Amos' visions? (v. 1)

    [5] You will flee by the valley of My mountains, for the valley of the mountains will reach to Azel; yes, you will flee just as you fled before the earthquake in the days of Uzziah king of Judah. Then the LORD, my God, will come, *and* all the holy ones with Him! (Zech. 14:5 NAU)

---

[5] Scherman, Nosson, Meir Zlotowitz, Sheah Brander, and Menachem Davis. "Amos." In *The Prophets: The Later Prophets with a Commentary Anthologized from the Rabbinic Writings*. Brooklyn, NY: Mesorah Publications, 2013.
[6] Bible Map: Tekoa. Accessed December 04, 2017. http://bibleatlas.org/tekoa.htm.

Zechariah the prophet attests to the earthquake, which was probably in the year 750 BCE and was at least a magnitude 8 quake.[7] Zachariah was a contemporary of Amos. Therefore, through Zechariah, a dating of Amos can be obtained.

4. Where was Carmel? (v. 2)

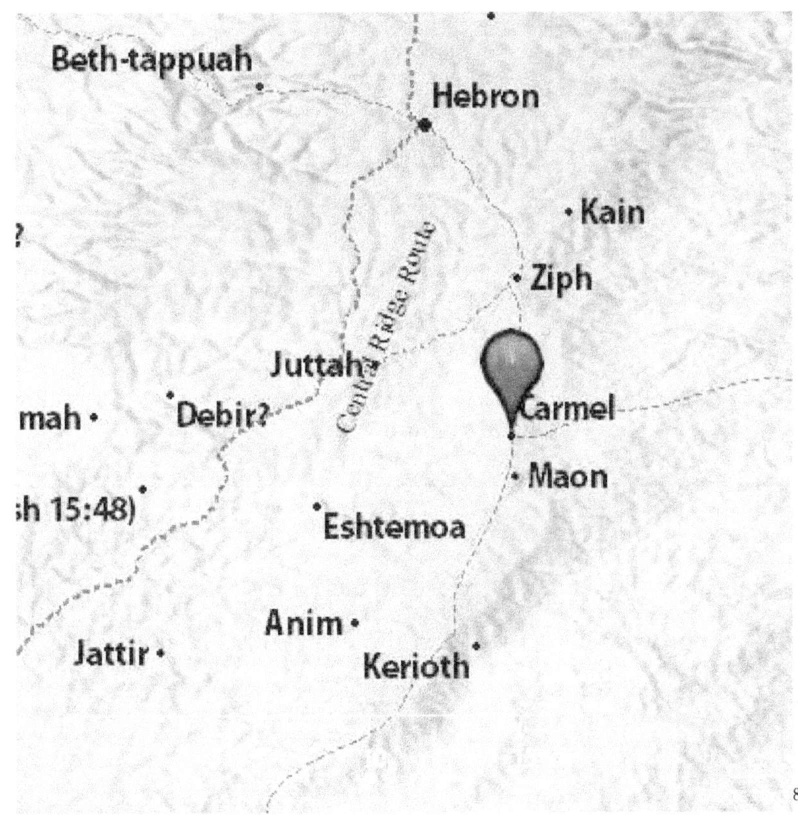

5. Is not Zion and Jerusalem the same place? (v. 2)

There is an emphasis found by repetition in the Hebrew Scriptures. Another way to understand this is that Zion is the mountain of the LORD while Jerusalem is God's city on God's mountain. The Sages tell us that when this expression is used, we are being told that the Shekinah of the LORD was shouting the vision to Amos. Amos' vision came from the LORD's Shekinah, which lived inside the Holy of Holies in the Temple in Jerusalem on top of Mount Zion.

---

[7] "The Scientific and Scriptural Impact of Amos' Earthquake." The Scientific and Scriptural Impact of Amos' Earthquake | The Institute for Creation Research. Accessed December 04, 2017. http://www.icr.org/article/scientific-scriptural-impact-amos-earthquake/. (Austin n.d.)
[8] Bible Map: Carmel. Accessed December 04, 2017. http://bibleatlas.org/carmel.htm.

6. Where was Gilead and what was its significance? (v. 3)

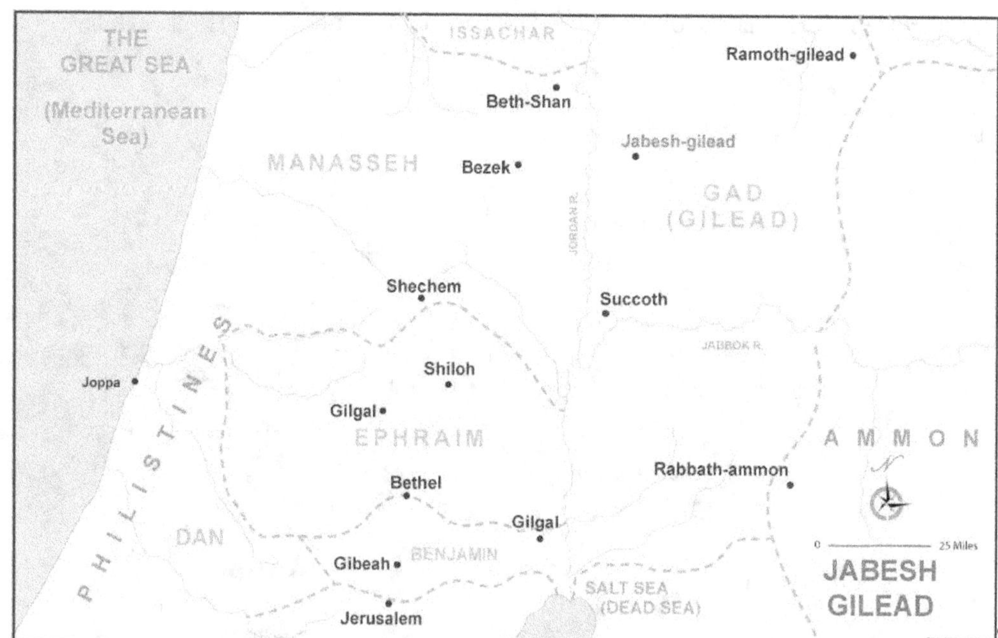

The people of Damascus (Syria) had come into the land of Gilead and tortured the Israelites who lived in that part of the country. They came to plunder the people and the land. Amos was telling them that the LORD was going to send His wrath upon them for what they did to God's Chosen People.

7. Who was Hazael? (v. 4)

   [15] The LORD said to him, "Go, return on your way to the wilderness of Damascus, and when you have arrived, you shall anoint Hazael king over Aram; (1 Ki. 19:15 NAU)

   1 Kings says that Hazael was the King over Aram. Damascus was a city in Aram (modern day Syria).

8. Where were the citadels of Ben-hadad and what were their significance? (v. 4)

   Ben Hadad was a king of Damascus at the same time as Hazael. There were two kings in Syria during Amos' time. The citadels of Ben-hadad are a reference to the palace of the king.

---

[9] Bible-history.com. "Books of the Bible Maps- Geography and the Bible (Bible History Online)." Bible History Online Images & Resource Pages. Accessed December 04, 2017. (Books of the Bible Maps n.d.).

9. Where was the valley of Aven? (v. 5)

The valley of Aven was another name for the town of Bethel.

10. Who is holding the scepter from Beth-eden? (v. 5)

The person holding the scepter was the King of Beth-Eden. Beth-Eden was another name

for Damascus.

---

10 Bible Map: Valley of Aven (Bethel). Accessed December 05, 2017. http://bibleatlas.org/valley_of_aven.htm.

11. Where was Beth_eden? (v. 5)

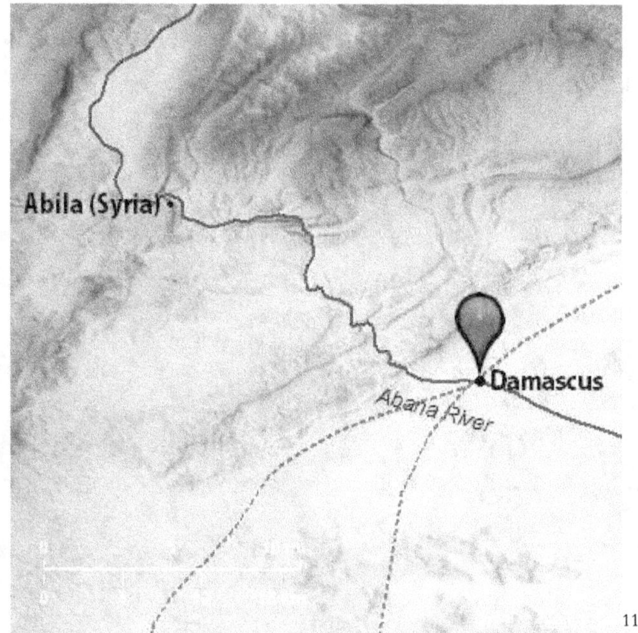

12. Who were the people of Aram? (v. 5)

Aram is another name for Syria.

13. Where was Kir? (v. 5)

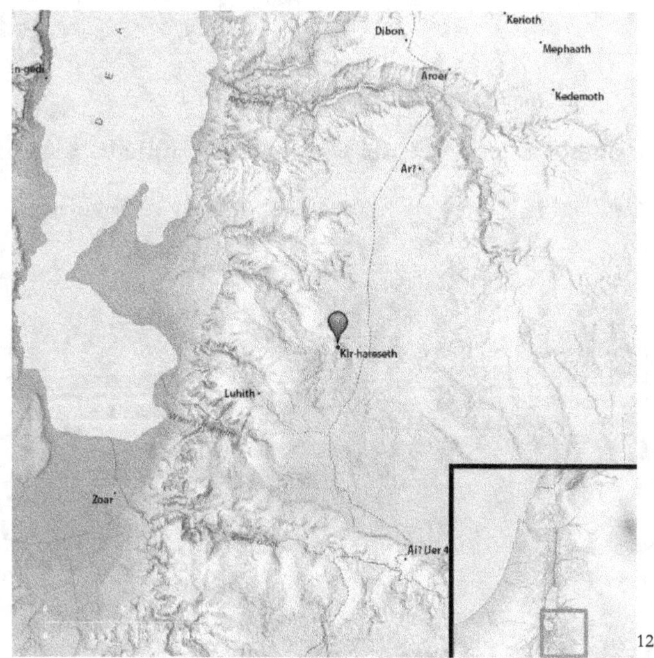

____

[11] Bible Map: Beth-eden (Damascus). Accessed December 05, 2017. http://bibleatlas.org/beth-eden.htm.
[12] Bible Map: Kir-hareseth (Kir). Accessed December 05, 2017. http://bibleatlas.org/full/kir-hareseth.htm.

14. Who were the people of Gaza? (v. 6)

    The Philistines lived in the city of Gaza and it was their capital city.

15. Why are the people of Gaza called the Philistines in verse 8?

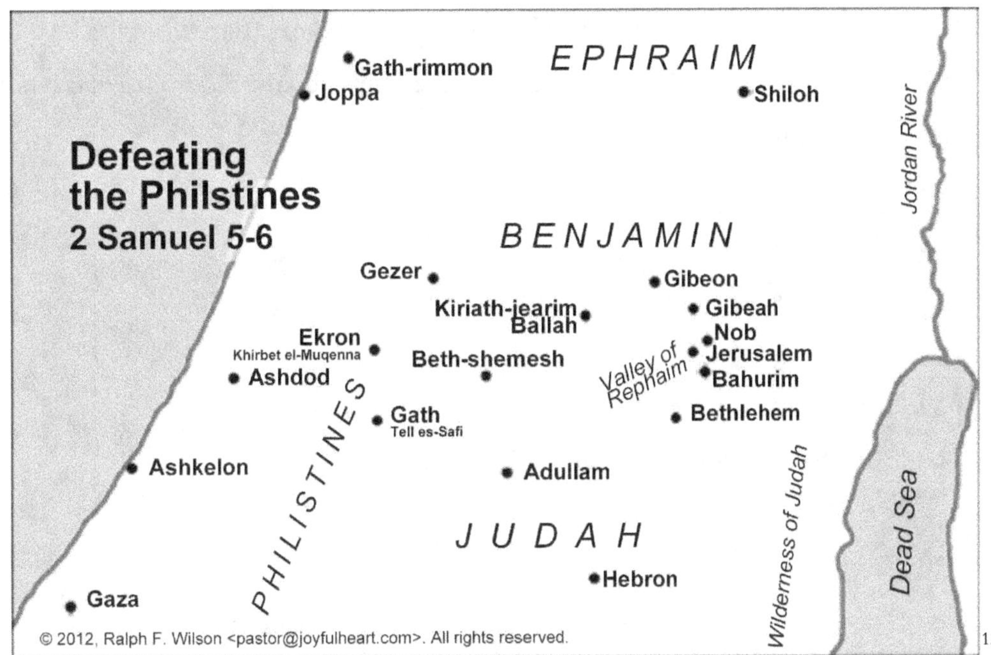

    The cities mentioned in this section are the cities of the Philistines. God calls out the destruction of each of the cities, then concludes this decision by using the name of the peoples who lived in the cities.

16. What was the covenant of brotherhood? (v. 9)

    A covenant was made between Hiram, King of Tyre and King Solomon (1 Kings 5:26). When the Romans invaded Judea, many people tried to escape the bloodshed by hiding in the land of Tyre. The leadership of Tyre captured many of the refugees and turned them over to the Roman government, who killed them. Amos prophesied that a day would come when the LORD would take vengeance on Tyre because of what they did to God's Chosen people.[14]

---

[13] Life of David: Maps and Graphics. Accessed December 05, 2017..

[14] Scherman, Nosson, Meir Zlotowitz, Sheah Brander, and Menachem Davis. "Amos." In *The Prophets: The Later Prophets with a Commentary Anthologized from the Rabbinic Writings*. Brooklyn, NY: Mesorah Publications, 2013.

17. Who were the brothers of Edom in verse 11?

The brothers of Edom refer to the brothers Esau and Jacob. For centuries, Edom (the descendants of Esau) attacked the Hebrews (the descendants of Jacob) living in Judah. When the Babylonians invaded Judah, many refugees tried to escape by going through the country of Edom. Many of them were captured by the Edomites and handed over to the Babylonians.

18. Where was Teman? (v. 12)

Teman was a city in the nation of Edom.

19. Where was Bozrah? (v. 12)

Bozrah was a city in the nation of Edom.

20. Who were the Ammonites? (v. 13)

The nations of Ammon and Moab were descendants of Lot, the nephew of Abraham. Therefore, the Ammonites were relatives of the Israelites. Despite this relationship, the Ammonites committed aggressions against Israel.[15]

21. What does the metaphor "they ripped open the pregnant women of Gilead" mean in verse 13?

In several translations, this phrase says, "they split the mountains of Gilead." What this means is the Ammonites attacked Gilead and enlarged their territory by annexing some of the territory of Gilead. The Torah has a reference about this:

[17] "Cursed be anyone who moves a neighbor's boundary marker." All the people shall say, "Amen!" (Deut. 27:17 NRS)

---

[15] IBID.

"Alternatively, הָרוֹת (Amos 1:13 WTT) refers to the fortified cities, depicted as mountains to symbolize their strength, which was conquered and razed by the people of Ammon (Radak[16])."[17]

22. Where was the wall of Rabbah? (v. 14)

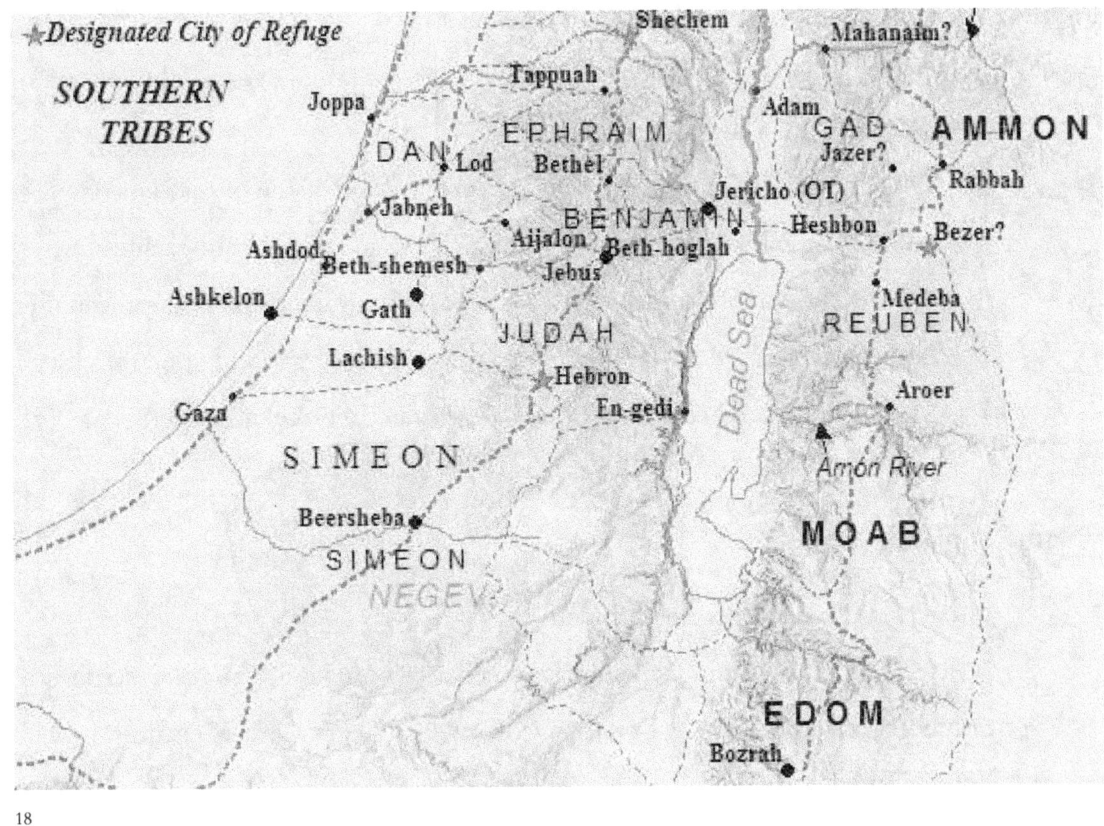

18

23. What does it mean to "kindle a fire against the wall?" (v. 14)

The LORD was saying through Amos that He was going to send an army to invade Ammon and to destroy its capital.

---

[16] Rabbi David Kimchi's father, Rabbi Joseph Ben Isaac Kimchi, lived in Southern Spain. His writings were among the first to introduce the study of Hebrew grammar and culture into Christian Europe. Under the cruel persecution of the Almohades, Rabbi Joseph Kimchi migrated north to Narbonne in France. He was born in 1160 CE. Source: (Rabbi David Kimchi - RaDaK n.d.)

[17] IBID.

[18] "Map of Palestine." Israel-a-history-of.com. Accessed December 08, 2017.

24. Why is the king and his officials mentioned in verse 15?

Not only will the nation of Ammon be overrun by an invading army, the king and his officials will be exiled from the land.[19]

People's names

1. עָמוֹס *Amos* **Meaning:** an Israeli prophet

2. עֻזִּיָּה *Uzziyyah* or עֻזִּיָּהוּ *Uzziyyahu* **Meaning:** 'my strength is Yah,' the name of several Israelites

3. יָרָבְעָם *Yarobam* **Meaning:** 'the people increase,' the name of two Israelite Kings

4. יְהוֹאָשׁ *Yehoash* **Meaning:** 'Yah is strong,' the name of several Israelites

5. בֶּן־הֲדָד *Ben-hadad* **Meaning:** 'son of Hadad,' the name of several Aramean (Syrian) kings

6. חֲזָאֵל *Chazael* or חֲזָהאֵל *Chazahel* **Meaning:** 'God sees,' a king of Aram (Syria)

7. בֵּית עֶדֶן *Beth Eden* **Meaning:** 'house of pleasure,' a place in Aram (Syria)

Name of places

1. תְּקוֹעַ *Teqoa* **Meaning:** a city in Judah

2. יְהוּדָה *Yehudah* **Meaning:** probably. 'praised,' a son of Jacob, also his description, the Southern kingdom, יְרוּשָׁלַם *Yerushalaim* or יְרוּשָׁלַיִם *Yerushalayim* **Meaning:** probably 'foundation of peace,' capital city of all Israel

3. כַּרְמֶל *Karmel* **Meaning:** a mountain promontory on the Mediterranean, also a city near Hebron

4. אָוֶן *Aven* **Meaning:** 'wickedness,' a contemptuous synonym for two places

5. גִּלְעָד *Gilad* **Meaning:** a region in Israel, also the name of several Israelites

6. בֵּית עֶדֶן *Beth Eden* **Meaning:** 'house of pleasure,' a place in Aram (Syria)

7. קִיר *Qir* **Meaning:** a place of exile in south Babylon

8. עַזָּה *Azzah* **Meaning:** a Philistine city

9. אֱדוֹם *Edom* **Meaning:** another name for Esau, older son of Isaac, also his description and their territory

---

[19] Scherman, Nosson, Meir Zlotowitz, Sheah Brander, and Menachem Davis. "Amos." In *The Prophets: The Later Prophets with a Commentary Anthologized from the Rabbinic Writings*. Brooklyn, NY: Mesorah Publications, 2013.

10. אַשְׁקְלוֹן *Ashqelon* **Meaning:** a city of the Philistines

11. אַשְׁדּוֹד *Ashdod* **Meaning:** a city of the Philistines

12. עֶקְרוֹן **Meaning:** a Philistine city

13. פְּלִשׁ *Pelishti* **Meaning:** inhabitants of Philistia

14. צֹר *Tsor* or צוֹר *Tsor* **Meaning:** a Phoenician city

15. בֵּימָן *Teman* **Meaning:** a northern district of Edom, also an Edomite chief

16. בָּצְרָה *Botsrah* **Meaning:** 'fortress,' a city in Edom, also one in Moab

17. גִּלְעָד *Gilad* **Meaning:** a region in Israel, also the name of several Israelites

18. רַבָּה *Rabbah* **Meaning:** two places in Israel

Scripture cross references

Verse 1	2Sa 14:2; Jer 6:1; 2Ch 26:1-23; Isa 1:1; 2Ki 14:23-29; Hos 1:1; Zec 14:5
Verse 3	Isa 8:4; Isa 17:1-3; Jer 49:23-27; Zec 9:1
Verse 4	1Ki 20:1; 2Ki 6:24
Verse 5	Jer 51:30; Lam 2:9; 2Ki 16:9;
Verse 6	1Sa 6:17; Jer 47:1, Jer 47:5; Zep 2:4; Eze 35:5; Oba 1:11
Verse 8	2Ch 26:6; Zec 9:6; Jer 47:5; Zep 2:4; Isa 14:29-31; Jer 47:1-7; Eze 25:16; Joe 3:4-8; Zep 2:4-7; Zec 9:5-7
Verse 14	Deu 3:11; 1Ch 20:1; Jer 49:2; Eze 21:22; Isa 29:6; Isa 30:30
Verse 15	Deu 3:11; 1Ch 20:1; Jer 49:2; Eze 21:22; Isa 29:6; Isa 30:30

Thoughts

The three cardinal sins, idolatry, murder and adultery are sins that the LORD will forgive the people who lived around the Hebrews. However, the fourth cardinal sin against the LORD is attacking His Chosen People. Each of the nations mentioned in this chapter had committed that sin. Therefore, the LORD had to punish each of them. For us today, we can see that the LORD will forgive us for our sins. Yeshua offers some additional teachings on sin that need to be augmented by the three cardinal sins. One additional sin that is unforgivable denies the existence of God. Yeshua called this blasphemy against the Holy Spirit (or the Shekinah). This sin is the same as attacking God's Chosen People.

Amos Chapter 2

Language

English	Hebrew
¹ Thus says the LORD, "For three transgressions of Moab and for four I will not revoke its *punishment*, Because he burned the bones of the king of Edom to lime. ² "So I will send fire upon Moab And it will consume the citadels of Kerioth; And Moab will die amid tumult, With war cries and the sound of a trumpet. ³ "I will also cut off the judge from her midst And slay all her princes with him," says the LORD. ⁴ Thus says the LORD, "For three transgressions of Judah and for four I will not revoke its *punishment*, Because they rejected the law of the LORD And have not kept His statutes; Their lies also have led them astray, Those after which their fathers walked. ⁵ "So I will send fire upon Judah And it will consume the citadels of Jerusalem." ⁶ Thus says the LORD, "For three transgressions of Israel and for four I will not revoke its *punishment*, Because they sell the righteous for money And the needy for a pair of sandals. ⁷ "These who pant after the *very* dust of the earth on the head of the helpless Also turn aside the way of the humble; And a man and his father resort to the same girl In order to profane My holy name. ⁸ "On garments taken as pledges they stretch out beside every altar, And in the house of their God they drink the wine of those who have been fined. ⁹ "Yet it was I who destroyed the Amorite before them, Though his height *was* like the height of cedars And he *was* strong as the oaks; I even destroyed his fruit above and his root below. ¹⁰ "It was I who brought you up from the land of Egypt, And I led you in the wilderness forty years That you might take possession of the land of the Amorite. ¹¹ "Then I raised up some of your sons to be prophets And some of your young men to be Nazirites. Is this not so, O sons of Israel?" declares the LORD. ¹² "But you made the Nazirites drink wine, And you commanded the prophets saying, 'You shall not prophesy!' ¹³ "Behold, I am weighted down beneath you As a wagon is weighted down when filled with sheaves.	¹ כֹּה אָמַר יְהֹוָה עַל־שְׁלֹשָׁה פִּשְׁעֵי מוֹאָב וְעַל־אַרְבָּעָה לֹא אֲשִׁיבֶנּוּ עַל־שָׂרְפוֹ עַצְמוֹת מֶלֶךְ־אֱדוֹם לַשִּׂיד: ² וְשִׁלַּחְתִּי־אֵשׁ בְּמוֹאָב וְאָכְלָה אַרְמְנוֹת הַקְּרִיּוֹת וּמֵת בְּשָׁאוֹן מוֹאָב בִּתְרוּעָה בְּקוֹל שׁוֹפָר: ³ וְהִכְרַתִּי שׁוֹפֵט מִקִּרְבָּהּ וְכָל־שָׂרֶיהָ אֶהֱרוֹג עִמּוֹ אָמַר יְהֹוָה: פ ⁴ כֹּה אָמַר יְהֹוָה עַל־שְׁלֹשָׁה פִּשְׁעֵי יְהוּדָה וְעַל־אַרְבָּעָה לֹא אֲשִׁיבֶנּוּ עַל־מָאֳסָם אֶת־תּוֹרַת יְהֹוָה וְחֻקָּיו לֹא שָׁמָרוּ וַיַּתְעוּם כִּזְבֵיהֶם אֲשֶׁר־הָלְכוּ אֲבוֹתָם אַחֲרֵיהֶם: ⁵ וְשִׁלַּחְתִּי אֵשׁ בִּיהוּדָה וְאָכְלָה אַרְמְנוֹת יְרוּשָׁלָם: פ ⁶ כֹּה אָמַר יְהֹוָה עַל־שְׁלֹשָׁה פִּשְׁעֵי יִשְׂרָאֵל וְעַל־אַרְבָּעָה לֹא אֲשִׁיבֶנּוּ עַל־מִכְרָם בַּכֶּסֶף צַדִּיק וְאֶבְיוֹן בַּעֲבוּר נַעֲלָיִם: ⁷ הַשֹּׁאֲפִים עַל־עֲפַר־אֶרֶץ בְּרֹאשׁ דַּלִּים וְדֶרֶךְ עֲנָוִים יַטּוּ וְאִישׁ וְאָבִיו יֵלְכוּ אֶל־הַנַּעֲרָה לְמַעַן חַלֵּל אֶת־שֵׁם קָדְשִׁי: ⁸ וְעַל־בְּגָדִים חֲבֻלִים יַטּוּ אֵצֶל כָּל־מִזְבֵּחַ וְיֵין עֲנוּשִׁים יִשְׁתּוּ בֵּית אֱלֹהֵיהֶם: ⁹ וְאָנֹכִי הִשְׁמַדְתִּי אֶת־הָאֱמֹרִי מִפְּנֵיהֶם אֲשֶׁר כְּגֹבַהּ אֲרָזִים גָּבְהוֹ וְחָסֹן הוּא כָּאַלּוֹנִים וָאַשְׁמִיד פִּרְיוֹ מִמַּעַל וְשָׁרָשָׁיו מִתָּחַת: ¹⁰ וְאָנֹכִי הֶעֱלֵיתִי אֶתְכֶם מֵאֶרֶץ מִצְרָיִם וָאוֹלֵךְ אֶתְכֶם בַּמִּדְבָּר אַרְבָּעִים שָׁנָה לָרֶשֶׁת אֶת־אֶרֶץ הָאֱמֹרִי: ¹¹ וָאָקִים מִבְּנֵיכֶם לִנְבִיאִים וּמִבַּחוּרֵיכֶם לִנְזִרִים הַאַף אֵין־זֹאת בְּנֵי יִשְׂרָאֵל נְאֻם־יְהֹוָה: ¹² וַתַּשְׁקוּ אֶת־הַנְּזִרִים יָיִן וְעַל־הַנְּבִיאִים צִוִּיתֶם לֵאמֹר לֹא תִּנָּבְאוּ:

¹⁴ "Flight will perish from the swift, And the stalwart will not strengthen his power, Nor the mighty man save his life.

¹⁵ "He who grasps the bow will not stand *his ground*, The swift of foot will not escape, Nor will he who rides the horse save his life.

¹⁶ "Even the bravest among the warriors will flee naked in that day," declares the LORD.

13 הִנֵּה אָנֹכִי מֵעִיק תַּחְתֵּיכֶם כַּאֲשֶׁר תָּעִיק הָעֲגָלָה הַמְלֵאָה לָהּ עָמִיר:

14 וְאָבַד מָנוֹס מִקָּל וְחָזָק לֹא־יְאַמֵּץ כֹּחוֹ וְגִבּוֹר לֹא־יְמַלֵּט נַפְשׁוֹ:

15 וְתֹפֵשׂ הַקֶּשֶׁת לֹא יַעֲמֹד וְקַל בְּרַגְלָיו לֹא יְמַלֵּט וְרֹכֵב הַסּוּס לֹא יְמַלֵּט נַפְשׁוֹ:

16 וְאַמִּיץ לִבּוֹ בַּגִּבּוֹרִים עָרוֹם יָנוּס בַּיּוֹם־הַהוּא נְאֻם־יְהוָה: פ

Process of Discovery

Linguistics Section

Linguistic Structure

[Moab] [1] Thus says the LORD, "For three transgressions of Moab and for four I will not revoke its *punishment*, Because he burned the bones of the king of Edom to lime. [2] "So I will send fire upon Moab And it will consume the citadels of Kerioth; And Moab will die amid tumult, With war cries and the sound of a trumpet. [3] "I will also cut off the judge from her midst And slay all her princes with him," says the LORD.

[Judah] [4] Thus says the LORD, "For three transgressions of Judah and for four I will not revoke its *punishment*, Because they rejected the law of the LORD And have not kept His statutes; Their lies also have led them astray, Those after which their fathers walked. [5] "So I will send fire upon Judah And it will consume the citadels of Jerusalem."

[Israel] [6] Thus says the LORD, "For three transgressions of Israel and for four I will not revoke its *punishment*, Because they sell the righteous for money And the needy for a pair of sandals. [7] "These who pant after the *very* dust of the earth on the head of the helpless Also turn aside the way of the humble; And a man and his father resort to the same girl In order to profane My holy name. [8] "On garments taken as pledges they stretch out beside every altar, And in the house of their God they drink the wine of those who have been fined. [9] "Yet it was I who destroyed the Amorite before them, Though his height *was* like the height of cedars And he *was* strong as the oaks; I even destroyed his fruit above and his root below. [10] "It was I who brought you up from the land of Egypt, And I led you in the wilderness forty years That you might take possession of the land of the Amorite. [11] "Then I raised up some of your sons to be prophets And some of your young men to be Nazirites. Is this not so, O sons of Israel?" declares the LORD. [12] "But you made the Nazirites drink wine, And you commanded the prophets saying, 'You shall not prophesy!' [13] "Behold, I am weighted down beneath you As a wagon is weighted down when filled with sheaves. [14] "Flight will perish from the swift, And the stalwart will not strengthen his power, Nor the mighty man save his life. [15] "He who grasps the bow will not stand *his ground*, The swift of foot will not escape, Nor will he who rides the horse save his life. [16] "Even the bravest among the warriors will flee naked in that day," declares the LORD.

Discussion

This chapter is a continuation of chapter one. Amos continues to tell the nations surrounding Israel and Judah that the LORD has pronounced a sentence of destruction upon them because of their acts. The chapter has a very in-depth discussion of the sins of the Northern Kingdom, Israel.

Questioning the Passage

1. What does it mean to take the King of Edom's bones and turn them into lime? (v. 1)

   The Targum of Amos says that the King of Edom's bones were burned and used to plaster the walls of the King of Moab's house. The LORD is telling Moab that this disrespect of royalty was the fourth transgression that required a punishment.

2. Where was Kerioth located? (v. 2)

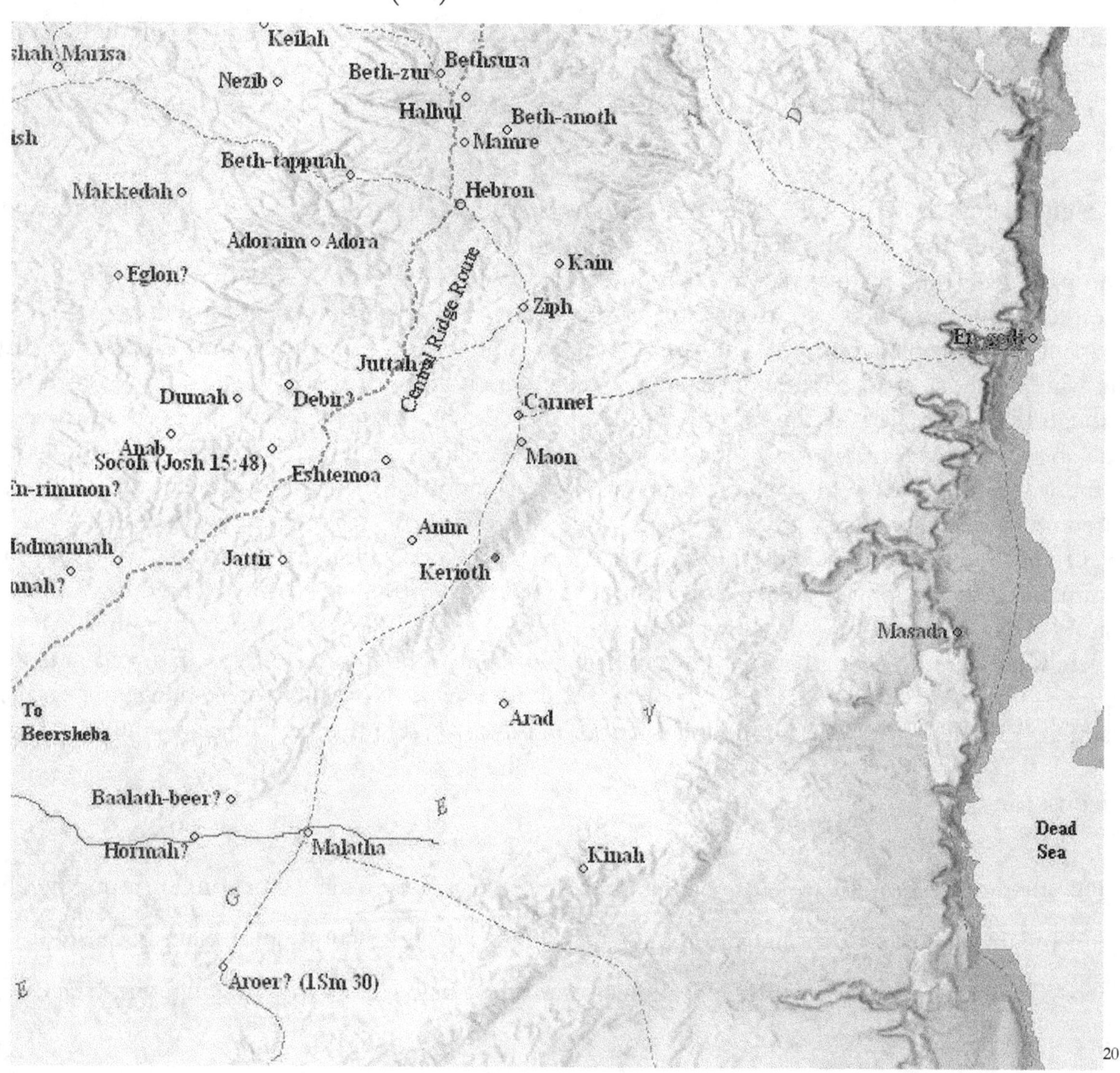

20 Horvat Kerioth. Accessed December 08, 2017. http://www.biblewalks.com/Sites/Kerioth.html.

3. What does it mean to "cut off" the judges in verse three?

    This expression means that the LORD was going to kill the judges, the people who maintained the government, with the king. Therefore, the nation of Moab would completely collapse.

4. What does "they sell the righteous for money and the needy for a pair of sandals (Amos 2:6 NAU)" mean?

    The Targum says that the people loathed the laws of the LORD and their leadership had led the people astray. The fourth sin for Judah was the corruption of the government and the worship of the LORD in His house. The corruption was so bad that judges were paid off to help the rich break the Laws of the LORD. The reference to the poor man's sandals was that the judges would rule harshly against the poor, so that everything they had would be given to rich people. There was a huge movement of wealth from the poor to the rich.[21]

5. What does it mean that a man and his father resort to the same girl? (v. 7)

    According to the Sage Rashi[22] this means that a man and his father would visit a brothel to have promiscuous relations with the same maiden at the same time.[23]

6. What does it mean to be stretched out in verse 8?

    The Targum says that the people went to the altars of the false gods, i.e. Baal, and worshiped these gods. The wine they were drinking was stolen.

7. What is the reference to the tall cedars in verse 9?

    The Amorites were the most powerful tribe in the Promised Land when the Israelites began the conquest. Amos is using the metaphor of the heights of the cedars to represent the power of the Amorite army. The LORD expected Israel to destroy the Amorites and their culture.

---

[21] Scherman, Nosson, Meir Zlotowitz, Sheah Brander, and Menachem Davis. "Amos." In *The Prophets: The Later Prophets with a Commentary Anthologized from the Rabbinic Writings*. Brooklyn, NY: Mesorah Publications, 2013.
[22] Rabbi Solomon ben Isaac (Shlomo Yitzhaki), known as Rashi (based on an acronym of his Hebrew initials), is one of the most influential Jewish commentators in history. He was born in Troyes, Champagne, in northern France, in 1040. Source: https://www.myjewishlearning.com/article/who-was-rashi/ (Rashi n.d.)
[23] IBID.

Instead, the Israelites adopted some ways of the Amorites, which led them away from worship to the LORD.[24]

8. What is the reference to the Nazarite drinking wine? (v. 12)

Nazarites were men who swore an allegiance to the LORD. They could not drink wine. The Nazarite code can be found in Numbers 6:1-21. Even the Nazarites broke their covenant with the LORD.

9. What does "flight will perish from the swift, And the stalwart will not strengthen his power, nor the mighty man save his life. (Amos 2:14 NAU)" means?

According to the Sage Rashi, this means that the people of Israel will be conquered by an army more powerful than they were. The LORD sent the Assyrians to conquer the Northern Kingdom. The army of the Northern Kingdom was no match for the army of the Assyrians. The Northern Kingdom created an alliance with Aram (Syria) but that did not stop the Assyrians. Verse 15 and 16 continue to tell the story that the army of the Northern Kingdom will not be a match for Assyria. Eventually, even the archers were overrun. The archers were usually behind the line of the foot soldiers because of the range the arrows had. The officers and the cavalry, the men on horseback, were eventually overtaken by Assyria.

People's names

1. יִשְׂרָאֵל *Yisrael* **Meaning:** 'God strives,' another name of Jacob and his descendants
2. יְהוּדָה *Yehudah* **Meaning:** probably 'praised,' a son of Jacob, also his description, the Southern kingdom, also four Isr.
3. אֱמֹרִי *Emori* **Meaning:** 'mountain dwellers,' a Canaanite tribe
4. מִצְרַיִם *Mitsrayim* **Meaning:** a son of Ham, also his descendants and their country in north west Africa

---

[24] IBID.

5. נָזִיר *nazir* or נָזִר *nazir* **Meaning:** *one consecrated, devoted* **Usage:** consecrated ones(1), Nazirite(9), Nazirites(2), one distinguished(2), untrimmed vines(2).

Name of places

1. אֱדוֹם *Edom* **Meaning:** another name for Esau, older son of Isaac, also his descendants and their territory

2. מוֹאָב *Moab* **Meaning:** a son of Lot, also his descendants and the territory where they settled

3. קְרִיּוֹת *Qeriyyoth* **Meaning:** a city in Judah, also a city in Moab

Scripture cross references

Verse 2	Jer 48:24, Jer 48:41, Jer 48:45
Verse 6	2Ki 18:11, 2Ki 18:12, Joe 3:3;
Verse 8	Exo 22:26
Verse 10	Exo 12:51; Exo 20:2; Deu 2:7; Exo 3:8
Verse 12	Exo 12:51; Exo 20:2; Deu 2:7, Exo 3:8
Verse 15	Jer 51:56; Eze 39:3. Isa 31:3

Culture Section

Discussion

In verse eight, there is a reference to pledged clothes. When money was lent by the rich, they often accepted clothing as collateral. The rich money lender who took the clothes as pledges kept them if the owner of the pledge failed to pay his debt.

Baal worshipers only drank old wine, which they considered better than new wine. They would get drunk, vomit and slept in their filthy garments in the houses of their gods or the houses of prostitution where the Baal worshipers met, ate and drank and committed sexual acts.[25]

---

[25] Errico, Rocco A., and George M. Lamsa. "Amos." In *Aramaic Light on Ezekiel, Daniel, and the Minor Prophets: A Commentary Based on the Aramaic Language and Ancient Near Eastern Customs*. Smyma, GA: Noohra Foundation, 2012.

Culture and Linguistics Discussion

The understanding of the cultural aspects of Baal worship assists in the understanding of verse 8 and what the fourth sin was. Some people of Israel had adopted the practices of Baal worship, especially drunkenness and prostitution. These acts were in violation of the LORD's word. When the people committed these acts, they were showing an allegiance to Baal and not to the LORD.

Thoughts

Regarding the condemnation of Israel (the Northern Kingdom), the fourth sin was adapting the cultural aspects of the land that they conquered, which took them away from their pledge to the LORD. In our society today, the culture of the United States has moved from being pro-God and pro-Yeshua, to anti-God and anti-Yeshua. Those who are disciples of Yeshua need to take extra care not to become a part of the culture which opposes the Laws of the LORD which are spelled out in the Scripture, and told us by Yeshua. It is not an easy task to stay away from the temptation of today's culture. But for the sake of your immortal soul, you need to stay under the wings of Yeshua and not submit to the evil that has become a part of our culture today.

Amos Chapter 3

Language

New American Standard 1995	Hebrew
[1] Hear this word which the LORD has spoken against you, sons of Israel, against the entire family which He brought up from the land of Egypt: [2] "You only have I chosen among all the families of the earth; Therefore I will punish you for all your iniquities." [3] Do two men walk together unless they have made an appointment? [4] Does a lion roar in the forest when he has no prey? Does a young lion growl from his den unless he has captured *something*? [5] Does a bird fall into a trap on the ground when there is no bait in it? Does a trap spring up from the earth when it captures nothing at all? [6] If a trumpet is blown in a city will not the people tremble? If a calamity occurs in a city has not the LORD done it? [7] Surely the Lord GOD does nothing Unless He reveals His secret counsel To His servants the prophets. [8] A lion has roared! Who will not fear? The Lord GOD has spoken! Who can but prophesy? [9] Proclaim on the citadels in Ashdod and on the citadels in the land of Egypt and say, "Assemble yourselves on the mountains of Samaria and see *the* great tumults within her and *the* oppressions in her midst. [10] "But they do not know how to do what is right," declares the LORD, "these who hoard up violence and devastation in their citadels." [11] Therefore, thus says the Lord GOD, "An enemy, even one surrounding the land, Will pull down your strength from you And your citadels will be looted." [12] Thus says the LORD, "Just as the shepherd snatches from the lion's mouth a couple of legs or a piece of an ear, So will the sons of Israel dwelling in Samaria be snatched away-- With *the* corner of a bed and *the* cover of a couch! [13] "Hear and testify against the house of Jacob," Declares the Lord GOD, the God of hosts. [14] "For on the day that I punish Israel's transgressions, I will also punish the altars of Bethel; The horns of the altar will be cut off And they will fall to the ground.	שִׁמְעוּ אֶת־הַדָּבָר הַזֶּה אֲשֶׁר דִּבֶּר יְהוָה עֲלֵיכֶם בְּנֵי יִשְׂרָאֵל עַל כָּל־הַמִּשְׁפָּחָה אֲשֶׁר הֶעֱלֵיתִי מֵאֶרֶץ מִצְרַיִם לֵאמֹר: ²רַק אֶתְכֶם יָדַעְתִּי מִכֹּל מִשְׁפְּחוֹת הָאֲדָמָה עַל־כֵּן אֶפְקֹד עֲלֵיכֶם אֵת כָּל־עֲוֺנֹתֵיכֶם: ³הֲיֵלְכוּ שְׁנַיִם יַחְדָּו בִּלְתִּי אִם־נוֹעָדוּ: ⁴הֲיִשְׁאַג אַרְיֵה בַּיַּעַר וְטֶרֶף אֵין לוֹ הֲיִתֵּן כְּפִיר קוֹלוֹ מִמְּעֹנָתוֹ בִּלְתִּי אִם־לָכָד: ⁵הֲתִפֹּל צִפּוֹר עַל־פַּח הָאָרֶץ וּמוֹקֵשׁ אֵין לָהּ הֲיַעֲלֶה־פַּח מִן־הָאֲדָמָה וְלָכוֹד לֹא יִלְכּוֹד: ⁶אִם־יִתָּקַע שׁוֹפָר בְּעִיר וְעָם לֹא יֶחֱרָדוּ אִם־תִּהְיֶה רָעָה בְּעִיר וַיהוָה לֹא עָשָׂה: ⁷כִּי לֹא יַעֲשֶׂה אֲדֹנָי יְהוִה דָּבָר כִּי אִם־גָּלָה סוֹדוֹ אֶל־עֲבָדָיו הַנְּבִיאִים: ⁸אַרְיֵה שָׁאָג מִי לֹא יִירָא אֲדֹנָי יְהוִה דִּבֶּר מִי לֹא יִנָּבֵא: ⁹הַשְׁמִיעוּ עַל־אַרְמְנוֹת בְּאַשְׁדּוֹד וְעַל־אַרְמְנוֹת בְּאֶרֶץ מִצְרָיִם וְאִמְרוּ הֵאָסְפוּ עַל־הָרֵי שֹׁמְרוֹן וּרְאוּ מְהוּמֹת רַבּוֹת בְּתוֹכָהּ וַעֲשׁוּקִים בְּקִרְבָּהּ: ¹⁰וְלֹא־יָדְעוּ עֲשׂוֹת־נְכֹחָה נְאֻם־יְהוָה הָאוֹצְרִים חָמָס וָשֹׁד בְּאַרְמְנוֹתֵיהֶם: פ ¹¹לָכֵן כֹּה אָמַר אֲדֹנָי יְהוִה צַר וּסְבִיב הָאָרֶץ וְהוֹרִד מִמֵּךְ עֻזֵּךְ וְנָבֹזּוּ אַרְמְנוֹתָיִךְ: ¹²כֹּה אָמַר יְהוָה כַּאֲשֶׁר יַצִּיל הָרֹעֶה מִפִּי הָאֲרִי שְׁתֵּי כְרָעַיִם אוֹ בְדַל־אֹזֶן כֵּן יִנָּצְלוּ בְּנֵי יִשְׂרָאֵל הַיֹּשְׁבִים בְּשֹׁמְרוֹן בִּפְאַת מִטָּה וּבִדְמֶשֶׁק עָרֶשׂ: ¹³שִׁמְעוּ וְהָעִידוּ בְּבֵית יַעֲקֹב נְאֻם־אֲדֹנָי יְהוִה אֱלֹהֵי הַצְּבָאוֹת: ¹⁴כִּי בְּיוֹם פָּקְדִי פִשְׁעֵי־יִשְׂרָאֵל עָלָיו וּפָקַדְתִּי עַל־מִזְבְּחוֹת בֵּית־אֵל וְנִגְדְּעוּ קַרְנוֹת הַמִּזְבֵּחַ וְנָפְלוּ לָאָרֶץ:

[15] "I will also smite the winter house together with the summer house; The houses of ivory will also perish And the great houses will come to an end," Declares the LORD.	וְהִכֵּיתִי בֵית־הַחֹרֶף עַל־בֵּית הַקָּיִץ וְאָבְדוּ [15] בָּתֵּי הַשֵּׁן וְסָפוּ בָּתִּים רַבִּים נְאֻם־יְהוָה׃ ס

Process of Discovery

Linguistics Section

Linguistic Structure

A [1] Hear this word which the LORD has spoken against you, sons of Israel, against the entire family which He brought up from the land of Egypt: [2] "You only have I chosen among all the families of the earth; Therefore I will punish you for all your iniquities."

> **B** [3] Do two men walk together unless they have made an appointment? [4] Does a lion roar in the forest when he has no prey? Does a young lion growl from his den unless he has captured *something*? [5] Does a bird fall into a trap on the ground when there is no bait in it? Does a trap spring up from the earth when it captures nothing at all? [6] If a trumpet is blown in a city will not the people tremble? If a calamity occurs in a city has not the LORD done it? [7] Surely the Lord GOD does nothing Unless He reveals His secret counsel To His servants the prophets. [8] A lion has roared! Who will not fear? The Lord GOD has spoken! Who can but prophesy?

>> **C** [9] Proclaim on the citadels in Ashdod and on the citadels in the land of Egypt and say, "Assemble yourselves on the mountains of Samaria and see *the* great tumults within her and *the* oppressions in her midst. [10] "But they do not know how to do what is right," declares the LORD, "these who hoard up violence and devastation in their citadels."

> **B'** [11] Therefore, thus says the Lord GOD, "An enemy, even one surrounding the land, Will pull down your strength from you And your citadels will be looted." [12] Thus says the LORD, "Just as the shepherd snatches from the lion's mouth a couple of legs or a piece of an ear, So will the sons of Israel dwelling in Samaria be snatched away-- With *the* corner of a bed and *the* cover of a couch!

A' [13] "Hear and testify against the house of Jacob," Declares the Lord GOD, the God of hosts. [14] "For on the day that I punish Israel's transgressions, I will also punish the altars of Bethel; The horns of the altar will be cut off And they will fall to the ground. [15] "I will also smite the winter house together with the summer house; The houses of ivory will also perish And the great houses will come to an end," Declares the LORD.

Discussion

This chapter is an A-B-C chiasm. The LORD is condemning, through Amos, the people in the Northern Kingdom of Israel.

Questioning the Passage

1. What is the curse proclaimed in verse 2?

    Since the people of Israel were given the Torah by the LORD, they should have known better about what displeases the LORD. However, the people acted just like the nations that surrounding them. Because the LORD gave the Torah to the people of Israel and they sinned, they received a more intensive punishment.

2. What do each of the metaphors mean in the chiasm's B block?[26]

    Seven rhetorical questions are offered by Amos.

    a. Do two men walk together unless they have made an appointment? (Amos 3:3 NAU)

        If two men walk together, it must mean that they know each other. When the words of the prophets come true, you know they were speaking the word of the LORD.

    b. Does a lion roar in the forest when he has no prey? (Amos 3:4 NAU)

        The lion's roar could be the Babylonians' victory roar when they defeated Judah and burned the city of Jerusalem.

    c. Does a young lion growl from his den unless he has captured something? (Amos 3:4 NAU)

        A young lion will not growl when he is in his den. Rather, he will growl and roar when he leaves the den and kills something.

    d. Does a bird fall into a trap on the ground when there is no bait in it? (Amos 3:5 NAU)

        Did the people believe they could commit sin without punishment? The bait is sin. A bird would not go into a trap on the ground if there was nothing to attract him.

    e. Does a trap spring up from the earth when it captures nothing at all? (Amos 3:5 NAU)

        When you sin, then a trap will close upon you. That trap is the punishment of the LORD. Therefore, it is better not to commit sin.

---

[26] Scherman, Nosson, Meir Zlotowitz, Sheah Brander, and Menachem Davis. "Amos." In *The Prophets: The Later Prophets with a Commentary Anthologized from the Rabbinic Writings*. Brooklyn, NY: Mesorah Publications, 2013.

f. If a trumpet is blown in a city, will not the people tremble? (Amos 3:6 NAU)

When a shofar (trumpet) was sounded, except on the required days, it signaled that an enemy was approaching the town. Unless an army was in the city await the enemy, the people would become afraid of what was going to happen to them.

g. If a calamity occurs in a city, has not the LORD done it? (Amos 3:6 NAU)

There are natural calamities that occur from time to time. The question here says that the LORD can bring calamity if He so desires it, especially upon a sinful city.

3. Why is the LORD calling for an assembly on the mountains of Samaria? (v. 9)

What the LORD is telling Amos is to tell the people of Samaria (another name for the Northern Kingdom of Israel) that their sins will cause the calamity that is about to come upon them.

4. In verse 12, the LORD refers to the sons of Israel while in verse 13 they are called the "house of Jacob." Why the change?

The sons of Israel refer to the Northern Kingdom, while the house of Jacob refers to the Southern Kingdom.

5. What does verse 12 means?

According to the Targum, this verse is hope to the people of Israel. As a shepherd will try with all his efforts to save a sheep from the clutches of a lion, the LORD will save a remnant of His people from the clutches of death.[27]

6. What is the reference to the altars of Bethel in verse 14?

The altars of Bethel were constructed in the Northern Kingdom for the worship of Baal and other false gods. The LORD says that He will not only punish the people, but He will also destroy anything built by the people to show honor to the pagan gods.

---

[27] IBID.

7. What is the winter house, summer house, house of ivory, and the great house? (v. 15)

These homes were owned by the wealthy people of the Northern Kingdom and the royalty. The LORD said that He will destroy them, so their wealth will not help them escape the punishment that was coming to the people of Israel.[28]

Main/Center Point

The main point of this chapter is the destruction of the Northern Kingdom of Israel. No one, rich or poor, could escape the punishment.

People's names

1. יִשְׂרָאֵל *Yisrael* **Meaning:** 'God strives,' another name of Jacob and his descendants

Name of places

1. מִצְרַיִם *Mitsrayim* **Meaning:** a son of Ham, also his descendants and their country in northwest Africa
2. אַשְׁדּוֹד *Ashdod* **Meaning:** a city of the Philistines
3. שֹׁמְרוֹן *Shomron* **Meaning:** capital of Northern kingdom of Israel
4. בֵּיתָאֵל *Betheel* **Meaning:** 'house of God,' a city in Ephraim, also a place in southern Judah

Scripture cross references

Verse 2	Gen 18:19; Exo 19:5, Exo 19:6; Deu 4:32-37; Deu 7:6; Jer 14:10; Eze 20:36; Dan 9:12; Rom 2:9
Verse 6	Gen 18:19; Exo 19:5, Exo 19:6; Deu 4:32-37; Deu 7:6; Jer 14:10; Eze 20:36; Dan 9:12; Rom 2:9
Verse 9	1 Sam 5:1
Verse 10	Psa 14:4; Jer 4:22; Hab 2:8-10; Zep 1:9; Zec 5:3, Zec 5:4
Verse 14	2Ki 23:15; Hos 10:5-8, Hos 10:14

---

[28] IBID.

Thoughts

It is clear from the chapter that Israel had to pay for her sins. The LORD gave Israel the Torah to be a guide for life to keep her away from sin. But they decided not to follow the LORD. They were influenced by the cultures around them. The LORD said through Amos that the people were still responsible for their actions. In today's culture in the United States, people like to blame everyone else for their behaviors and problems. Blaming parents, teachers, religious institutions, and schools seems to be the answer. The LORD says that ultimately each of us will be held accountable for our actions. You always have a choice, become like the cultural influence or look to the LORD and a better way of life.

Amos Chapter 4

Language

New American Standard 1995	Hebrew
¹ Hear this word, you cows of Bashan who are on the mountain of Samaria, Who oppress the poor, who crush the needy, Who say to your husbands, "Bring now, that we may drink!" ² The Lord GOD has sworn by His holiness, "Behold, the days are coming upon you When they will take you away with meat hooks, And the last of you with fish hooks. ³ "You will go out *through* breaches *in the walls*, Each one straight before her, And you will be cast to Harmon," declares the LORD. ⁴ "Enter Bethel and transgress; In Gilgal multiply transgression! Bring your sacrifices every morning, Your tithes every three days. ⁵ "Offer a thank offering also from that which is leavened, And proclaim freewill offerings, make them known. For so you love *to do*, you sons of Israel," Declares the Lord GOD. ⁶ "But I gave you also cleanness of teeth in all your cities And lack of bread in all your places, Yet you have not returned to Me," declares the LORD. ⁷ "Furthermore, I withheld the rain from you While *there were* still three months until harvest. Then I would send rain on one city And on another city I would not send rain; One part would be rained on, While the part not rained on would dry up. ⁸ "So two or three cities would stagger to another city to drink water, But would not be satisfied; Yet you have not returned to Me," declares the LORD. ⁹ "I smote you with scorching *wind* and mildew; And the caterpillar was devouring Your many gardens and vineyards, fig trees and olive trees; Yet you have not returned to Me," declares the LORD. ¹⁰ "I sent a plague among you after the manner of Egypt; I slew your young men by the sword along with your captured horses, And I made the stench of your camp rise up in your nostrils; Yet you have not returned to Me," declares the LORD. ¹¹ "I overthrew you, as God overthrew Sodom and Gomorrah, And you were like a firebrand snatched from a blaze; Yet you have not returned to Me," declares the LORD. ¹² "Therefore thus I will do to you, O Israel; Because I will do this to you, Prepare to meet your God, O Israel."	שִׁמְעוּ הַדָּבָר הַזֶּה פָּרוֹת הַבָּשָׁן אֲשֶׁר בְּהַר שֹׁמְרוֹן הָעֹשְׁקוֹת דַּלִּים הָרֹצְצוֹת אֶבְיוֹנִים הָאֹמְרֹת לַאֲדֹנֵיהֶם הָבִיאָה וְנִשְׁתֶּה׃ נִשְׁבַּע אֲדֹנָי יְהוִה בְּקָדְשׁוֹ כִּי הִנֵּה יָמִים בָּאִים עֲלֵיכֶם וְנִשָּׂא אֶתְכֶם בְּצִנּוֹת וְאַחֲרִיתְכֶן בְּסִירוֹת דּוּגָה׃ וּפְרָצִים תֵּצֶאנָה אִשָּׁה נֶגְדָּהּ וְהִשְׁלַכְתֶּנָה הַהַרְמוֹנָה נְאֻם־יְהוָה׃ בֹּאוּ בֵית־אֵל וּפִשְׁעוּ הַגִּלְגָּל הַרְבּוּ לִפְשֹׁעַ וְהָבִיאוּ לַבֹּקֶר זִבְחֵיכֶם לִשְׁלֹשֶׁת יָמִים מַעְשְׂרֹתֵיכֶם׃ וְקַטֵּר מֵחָמֵץ תּוֹדָה וְקִרְאוּ נְדָבוֹת הַשְׁמִיעוּ כִּי כֵן אֲהַבְתֶּם בְּנֵי יִשְׂרָאֵל נְאֻם אֲדֹנָי יְהוִה׃ וְגַם־אֲנִי נָתַתִּי לָכֶם נִקְיוֹן שִׁנַּיִם בְּכָל־עָרֵיכֶם וְחֹסֶר לֶחֶם בְּכֹל מְקוֹמֹתֵיכֶם וְלֹא־שַׁבְתֶּם עָדַי נְאֻם־יְהוָה׃ וְגַם אָנֹכִי מָנַעְתִּי מִכֶּם אֶת־הַגֶּשֶׁם בְּעוֹד שְׁלֹשָׁה חֳדָשִׁים לַקָּצִיר וְהִמְטַרְתִּי עַל־עִיר אֶחָת וְעַל־עִיר אַחַת לֹא אַמְטִיר חֶלְקָה אַחַת תִּמָּטֵר וְחֶלְקָה אֲשֶׁר־לֹא־תַמְטִיר עָלֶיהָ תִּיבָשׁ׃ וְנָעוּ שְׁתַּיִם שָׁלֹשׁ עָרִים אֶל־עִיר אַחַת לִשְׁתּוֹת מַיִם וְלֹא יִשְׂבָּעוּ וְלֹא־שַׁבְתֶּם עָדַי נְאֻם־יְהוָה׃ הִכֵּיתִי אֶתְכֶם בַּשִּׁדָּפוֹן וּבַיֵּרָקוֹן הַרְבּוֹת גַּנּוֹתֵיכֶם וְכַרְמֵיכֶם וּתְאֵנֵיכֶם וְזֵיתֵיכֶם יֹאכַל הַגָּזָם וְלֹא־שַׁבְתֶּם עָדַי נְאֻם־יְהוָה׃ ס שִׁלַּחְתִּי בָכֶם דֶּבֶר בְּדֶרֶךְ מִצְרַיִם הָרַגְתִּי בַחֶרֶב בַּחוּרֵיכֶם עִם שְׁבִי סוּסֵיכֶם וָאַעֲלֶה בְּאֹשׁ מַחֲנֵיכֶם וּבְאַפְּכֶם וְלֹא־שַׁבְתֶּם עָדַי נְאֻם־יְהוָה׃

<table>
<tr>
<td>

13 For behold, He who forms mountains and creates the wind And declares to man what are His thoughts, He who makes dawn into darkness And treads on the high places of the earth, The LORD God of hosts is His name.

</td>
<td dir="rtl">

11 הֲפַכְתִּי בָכֶם כְּמַהְפֵּכַת אֱלֹהִים אֶת־סְדֹם וְאֶת־עֲמֹרָה וַתִּהְיֹוּ כְּאוּד מֻצָּל מִשְׂרֵפָה וְלֹא־שַׁבְתֶּם עָדַי נְאֻם־יְהוָה: ס

12 לָכֵן כֹּה אֶעֱשֶׂה־לְּךָ יִשְׂרָאֵל עֵקֶב כִּי־זֹאת אֶעֱשֶׂה־לָּךְ הִכֹּון לִקְרַאת־אֱלֹהֶיךָ יִשְׂרָאֵל:

13 כִּי הִנֵּה יוֹצֵר הָרִים וּבֹרֵא רוּחַ וּמַגִּיד לְאָדָם מַה־שֵּׂחֹו עֹשֵׂה שַׁחַר עֵיפָה וְדֹרֵךְ עַל־בָּמֳתֵי אָרֶץ יְהוָה אֱלֹהֵי־צְבָאֹות שְׁמֹו: ס

</td>
</tr>
</table>

Process of Discovery

Linguistics Section

Linguistic Structure

[Proclamation 1][1] Hear this word, you cows of Bashan who are on the mountain of Samaria, Who oppress the poor, who crush the needy, Who say to your husbands, "Bring now, that we may drink!" [2] The Lord GOD has sworn by His holiness, "Behold, the days are coming upon you When they will take you away with meat hooks, And the last of you with fish hooks. [3] "You will go out *through* breaches *in the walls*, Each one straight before her, And you will be cast to Harmon," declares the LORD. [4] "Enter Bethel and transgress; In Gilgal multiply transgression! Bring your sacrifices every morning, Your tithes every three days. [5] "Offer a thank offering also from that which is leavened, And proclaim freewill offerings, make them known. For so you love *to do*, you sons of Israel," Declares the Lord GOD.

[Proclamation 2] [6] "But I gave you also cleanness of teeth in all your cities And lack of bread in all your places, Yet you have not returned to Me," declares the LORD.

[Proclamation 3] [7] "Furthermore, I withheld the rain from you While *there were* still three months until harvest. Then I would send rain on one city And on another city I would not send rain; One part would be rained on, While the part not rained on would dry up. [8] "So two or three cities would stagger to another city to drink water, But would not be satisfied; Yet you have not returned to Me," declares the LORD.

[Proclamation 4] [9] "I smote you with scorching *wind* and mildew; And the caterpillar was devouring Your many gardens and vineyards, fig trees and olive trees; Yet you have not returned to Me," declares the LORD.

[Proclamation 5][10] "I sent a plague among you after the manner of Egypt; I slew your young men by the sword along with your captured horses, And I made the stench of your camp rise up in your nostrils; Yet you have not returned to Me," declares the LORD.

[Proclamation 6] [11] "I overthrew you, as God overthrew Sodom and Gomorrah, And you were like a firebrand snatched from a blaze; Yet you have not returned to Me," declares the LORD.

[Proclamation 7] [12] "Therefore thus I will do to you, O Israel; Because I will do this to you, Prepare to meet your God, O Israel." [13] For behold, He who forms mountains and creates the wind And declares to man what are His thoughts, He who makes dawn into darkness And treads on the high places of the earth, The LORD God of hosts is His name.

Discussion

This chapter is a list of proclamations that the LORD makes against the Northern Kingdom of Israel.

Questioning the Passage

(The questions and answers offered are for discussion. You may have different questions and answers. Remember, all questions are valid and all answers must be defendable from Scripture. This applies to this section and to the Culture Section.)

1. Who are the cows of Bashan who live on the mountains of Samaria? (v. 1)

   The Targum says that the rich of Samaria are about to be punished for their wicked ways. The Sage Radak said that this chapter is the LORD talking to the women of the rich men of Israel. They were self-indulgent and beautiful from pampering themselves. The women are being accused of pushing their husbands into oppressing the poor because they constantly needed more money and luxuries to satisfy their wives.[29]

   "(1) **Bashan.**—This contained the rich pasture-lands east of the Jordan, between Hermon and the mountains of Gilead, where cattle flourished. The "strong bulls of Bashan" (Psalm 22:12) were descriptive of the malignant enemies of the ideal sufferer. The feminine "kine" refers to the luxurious self-indulgent women of fashion in Samaria."[30]

2. What is the meaning of the metaphor "meat hooks" and "fish hooks?" (v. 2)

---

[29] Scherman, Nosson, Meir Zlotowitz, Sheah Brander, and Menachem Davis. "Amos." In *The Prophets: The Later Prophets with a Commentary Anthologized from the Rabbinic Writings*. Brooklyn, NY: Mesorah Publications, 2013.
[30] Amos 4:1 Commentaries: Hear This Word, You Cows of Bashan Who Are on the Mountain of Samaria, Who Oppress the Poor, Who Crush the Needy, Who Say to Your Husbands, "Bring Now, That We May Drink!" Accessed December 11, 2017.

The Targum says that the LORD was telling the women that one day an enemy would come to their cities, break down the walls, and carry them away on their shields. Their daughters would be taken away from the cities in the enemy's fishing boats.

3. What does it mean to be cast to Harmon? (v. 3)

   The LORD tells the women that they will be taken out of their cities through the breaches in the walls that were created by the invading army. They would be taken far away from their homeland. Being cast to Harmon, according to the Targum, means that they will be taken far north of Armenia.

4. What are the transgressions of Bethel and Gilgal? (v. 4)

   The women continued their worshiping of the pagan gods, including bringing sacrifices before the pagan gods even through the are fully aware that what they are doing was idolatry and only angered the LORD.

5. What is the cleanness of teeth? (v. 6)

   This is a metaphor, so the LORD was going to cause such a famine that the women would not have meat to eat. The calamities that the LORD brought upon the people of Israel are expressed through the rest of the chapter.

Main/Center Point

In this chapter, the LORD's attention is focused on the women of Israel. Amos tells them that the LORD blames them for the corruption of their men. The rich women demanded so many luxuries that their husbands were forced to oppress the poor of the country to gather the monies needed to keep their wives happy. The LORD tells the women that they will suffer a similar fate as their husbands regarding the punishment from the LORD.

Name of places
1. בָּשָׁן *Bashan* **Meaning:** 'smooth,' a region east of the Jordan

2. שֹׁמְרוֹן *Shomron* **Meaning:** capital of northern kingdom of Israel

3. הַרְמוֹן *Harmon* **Meaning:** a place name

4. גִּלְגָּל *Gilgal* **Meaning:** 'circle (of stones),' the name of several places in Palestine

5. בֵּיתָאֵל *Betheel* **Meaning:** 'house of God,' a city in Ephraim, also a place in southern Judah

6. סְדֹם *Sedom* **Meaning:** a Canaanite city near the Dead Sea

7. עֲמֹרָה *Amorah* **Meaning:** a city in the Jordan Valley

8. מִצְרַיִם *Mitsrayim* **Meaning:** a son of Ham, also his descendants and their country in northwest Africa

9. יִשְׂרָאֵל *Yisrael* **Meaning:** 'God strives,' another name of Jacob and his descendants

Scripture cross references

Verse 3	Jer 52:7
Verse 4	Isa 3:1; Jer 14:18; Isa 9:13; Jer 5:3; Hag 2:17
Verse 5	Isa 3:1; Jer 14:18; Isa 9:13; Jer 5:3; Hag 2:17
Verse 6	Isa 3:1; Jer 14:18; Isa 9:13; Jer 5:3; Hag 2:17
Verse 8	1Ki 18:5; Jer 14:4; Eze 4:16, Eze 4:17; Hag 1:6; Jer 3:7
Verse 9	Deu 28:22; Hag 2:17, Joe 1:4, Joe 1:7; Jer 3:10
Verse 10	Exo 9:3; Lev 26:25; Deu 28:27, Deu 28:60; Psa 78:50; Jer 11:22; Jer 18:21; Jer 48:15; 2Ki 13:3, 2Ki 13:7; Joe 2:20; Isa 9:13

Thoughts

Perhaps the women in Amos' day did not believe that they were contributing to the immorality of the day when indeed they were a cause of the problem. Greed can always have an influence on our behavior and attitudes. We need to recognize that greed exists and that we must not allow it to take us away from our love and devotion to the LORD.

Amos Chapter 5

Language

New American Standard 1995	Hebrew
1 Hear this word which I take up for you as a dirge, O house of Israel: 2 She has fallen, she will not rise again-- The virgin Israel. She *lies* neglected on her land; There is none to raise her up. 3 For thus says the Lord GOD, "The city which goes forth a thousand *strong* Will have a hundred left, And the one which goes forth a hundred *strong* Will have ten left to the house of Israel." 4 For thus says the LORD to the house of Israel, "Seek Me that you may live. 5 "But do not resort to Bethel And do not come to Gilgal, Nor cross over to Beersheba; For Gilgal will certainly go into captivity And Bethel will come to trouble. 6 "Seek the LORD that you may live, Or He will break forth like a fire, O house of Joseph, And it will consume with none to quench *it* for Bethel, 7 *For* those who turn justice into wormwood And cast righteousness down to the earth." 8 He who made the Pleiades and Orion And changes deep darkness into morning, Who also darkens day *into* night, Who calls for the waters of the sea And pours them out on the surface of the earth, The LORD is His name. 9 It is He who flashes forth *with* destruction upon the strong, So that destruction comes upon the fortress. 10 They hate him who reproves in the gate, And they abhor him who speaks *with* integrity. 11 Therefore because you impose heavy rent on the poor And exact a tribute of grain from them, *Though* you have built houses of well-hewn stone, Yet you will not live in them; You have planted pleasant vineyards, yet you will not drink their wine. 12 For I know your transgressions are many and your sins are great, *You* who distress the righteous *and* accept bribes And turn aside the poor in the gate. 13 Therefore at such a time the prudent person keeps silent, for it is an evil time. 14 Seek good and not evil, that you may live; And thus may the LORD God of hosts be with you, Just as you have said!	1 שִׁמְעוּ אֶת־הַדָּבָר הַזֶּה אֲשֶׁר אָנֹכִי נֹשֵׂא עֲלֵיכֶם קִינָה בֵּית יִשְׂרָאֵל: 2 נָפְלָה לֹא־תוֹסִיף קוּם בְּתוּלַת יִשְׂרָאֵל נִטְּשָׁה עַל־אַדְמָתָהּ אֵין מְקִימָהּ: 3 כִּי כֹה אָמַר אֲדֹנָי יְהוִֹה הָעִיר הַיֹּצֵאת אֶלֶף תַּשְׁאִיר מֵאָה וְהַיּוֹצֵאת מֵאָה תַּשְׁאִיר עֲשָׂרָה לְבֵית יִשְׂרָאֵל: ס 4 כִּי כֹה אָמַר יְהוָה לְבֵית יִשְׂרָאֵל דִּרְשׁוּנִי וִחְיוּ: 5 וְאַל־תִּדְרְשׁוּ בֵּית־אֵל וְהַגִּלְגָּל לֹא תָבֹאוּ וּבְאֵר שֶׁבַע לֹא תַעֲבֹרוּ כִּי הַגִּלְגָּל גָּלֹה יִגְלֶה וּבֵית־אֵל יִהְיֶה לְאָוֶן: 6 דִּרְשׁוּ אֶת־יְהוָה וִחְיוּ פֶּן־יִצְלַח כָּאֵשׁ בֵּית יוֹסֵף וְאָכְלָה וְאֵין־מְכַבֶּה לְבֵית־אֵל: 7 הַהֹפְכִים לְלַעֲנָה מִשְׁפָּט וּצְדָקָה לָאָרֶץ הִנִּיחוּ: 8 עֹשֵׂה כִימָה וּכְסִיל וְהֹפֵךְ לַבֹּקֶר צַלְמָוֶת וְיוֹם לַיְלָה הֶחְשִׁיךְ הַקּוֹרֵא לְמֵי־הַיָּם וַיִּשְׁפְּכֵם עַל־פְּנֵי הָאָרֶץ יְהוָה שְׁמוֹ: ס 9 הַמַּבְלִיג שֹׁד עַל־עָז וְשֹׁד עַל־מִבְצָר יָבוֹא: 10 שָׂנְאוּ בַשַּׁעַר מוֹכִיחַ וְדֹבֵר תָּמִים יְתָעֵבוּ: 11 לָכֵן יַעַן בּוֹשַׁסְכֶם עַל־דָּל וּמַשְׂאַת־בַּר תִּקְחוּ מִמֶּנּוּ בָּתֵּי גָזִית בְּנִיתֶם וְלֹא־תֵשְׁבוּ בָם כַּרְמֵי־חֶמֶד נְטַעְתֶּם וְלֹא תִשְׁתּוּ אֶת־יֵינָם: 12 כִּי יָדַעְתִּי רַבִּים פִּשְׁעֵיכֶם וַעֲצֻמִים חַטֹּאתֵיכֶם צֹרְרֵי צַדִּיק לֹקְחֵי כֹפֶר וְאֶבְיוֹנִים בַּשַּׁעַר הִטּוּ: 13 לָכֵן הַמַּשְׂכִּיל בָּעֵת הַהִיא יִדֹּם כִּי עֵת רָעָה הִיא: 14 דִּרְשׁוּ־טוֹב וְאַל־רָע לְמַעַן תִּחְיוּ וִיהִי־כֵן יְהוָה אֱלֹהֵי־צְבָאוֹת אִתְּכֶם כַּאֲשֶׁר אֲמַרְתֶּם:

¹⁵ Hate evil, love good, And establish justice in the gate! Perhaps the LORD God of hosts May be gracious to the remnant of Joseph.

¹⁶ Therefore thus says the LORD God of hosts, the Lord, "There is wailing in all the plazas, And in all the streets they say, 'Alas! Alas!' They also call the farmer to mourning And professional mourners to lamentation.

¹⁷ "And in all the vineyards *there is* wailing, Because I will pass through the midst of you," says the LORD.

¹⁸ Alas, you who are longing for the day of the LORD, For what purpose *will* the day of the LORD *be* to you? It *will be* darkness and not light;

¹⁹ As when a man flees from a lion And a bear meets him, Or goes home, leans his hand against the wall And a snake bites him.

²⁰ *Will* not the day of the LORD *be* darkness instead of light, Even gloom with no brightness in it?

²¹ "I hate, I reject your festivals, Nor do I delight in your solemn assemblies.

²² "Even though you offer up to Me burnt offerings and your grain offerings, I will not accept *them*; And I will not *even* look at the peace offerings of your fatlings.

²³ "Take away from Me the noise of your songs; I will not even listen to the sound of your harps.

²⁴ "But let justice roll down like waters And righteousness like an ever-flowing stream.

²⁵ "Did you present Me with sacrifices and grain offerings in the wilderness for forty years, O house of Israel?

²⁶ "You also carried along Sikkuth your king and Kiyyun, your images, the star of your gods which you made for yourselves.

²⁷ "Therefore, I will make you go into exile beyond Damascus," says the LORD, whose name is the God of hosts.

¹⁵ שִׂנְאוּ־רָע וְאֶהֱבוּ טוֹב וְהַצִּיגוּ בַשַּׁעַר מִשְׁפָּט אוּלַי יֶחֱנַן יְהוָה אֱלֹהֵי־צְבָאוֹת שְׁאֵרִית יוֹסֵף: ס

¹⁶ לָכֵן כֹּה־אָמַר יְהוָה אֱלֹהֵי צְבָאוֹת אֲדֹנָי בְּכָל־רְחֹבוֹת מִסְפֵּד וּבְכָל־חוּצוֹת יֹאמְרוּ הוֹ־הוֹ וְקָרְאוּ אִכָּר אֶל־אֵבֶל וּמִסְפֵּד אֶל־יוֹדְעֵי נֶהִי:

¹⁷ וּבְכָל־כְּרָמִים מִסְפֵּד כִּי־אֶעֱבֹר בְּקִרְבְּךָ אָמַר יְהוָה: ס

¹⁸ הוֹי הַמִּתְאַוִּים אֶת־יוֹם יְהוָה לָמָּה־זֶּה לָכֶם יוֹם יְהוָה הוּא־חֹשֶׁךְ וְלֹא־אוֹר:

¹⁹ כַּאֲשֶׁר יָנוּס אִישׁ מִפְּנֵי הָאֲרִי וּפְגָעוֹ הַדֹּב וּבָא הַבַּיִת וְסָמַךְ יָדוֹ עַל־הַקִּיר וּנְשָׁכוֹ הַנָּחָשׁ:

²⁰ הֲלֹא־חֹשֶׁךְ יוֹם יְהוָה וְלֹא־אוֹר וְאָפֵל וְלֹא־נֹגַהּ לוֹ:

²¹ שָׂנֵאתִי מָאַסְתִּי חַגֵּיכֶם וְלֹא אָרִיחַ בְּעַצְּרֹתֵיכֶם:

²² כִּי אִם־תַּעֲלוּ־לִי עֹלוֹת וּמִנְחֹתֵיכֶם לֹא אֶרְצֶה וְשֶׁלֶם מְרִיאֵיכֶם לֹא אַבִּיט:

²³ הָסֵר מֵעָלַי הֲמוֹן שִׁרֶיךָ וְזִמְרַת נְבָלֶיךָ לֹא אֶשְׁמָע:

²⁴ וְיִגַּל כַּמַּיִם מִשְׁפָּט וּצְדָקָה כְּנַחַל אֵיתָן:

²⁵ הַזְּבָחִים וּמִנְחָה הִגַּשְׁתֶּם־לִי בַמִּדְבָּר אַרְבָּעִים שָׁנָה בֵּית יִשְׂרָאֵל:

²⁶ וּנְשָׂאתֶם אֵת סִכּוּת מַלְכְּכֶם וְאֵת כִּיּוּן צַלְמֵיכֶם כּוֹכַב אֱלֹהֵיכֶם אֲשֶׁר עֲשִׂיתֶם לָכֶם:

²⁷ וְהִגְלֵיתִי אֶתְכֶם מֵהָלְאָה לְדַמָּשֶׂק אָמַר יְהוָה אֱלֹהֵי־צְבָאוֹת שְׁמוֹ: פ

Process of Discovery

Linguistics Section

Linguistic Structure

A ^{Chapter 4:12} "Therefore thus I will do to you, O Israel; Because I will do this to you, Prepare to meet your God, O Israel." ¹³ For behold, He who forms mountains and creates the wind And declares to man what are His thoughts, He who makes dawn into darkness And treads on the high places of the earth, The LORD God of hosts is His name.

B ^{Chapter5:1} Hear this word which I take up for you as a dirge, O house of Israel: ² She has fallen, she will not rise again-- The virgin Israel. She *lies* neglected on her land; There is none to raise her up.

    C ³ For thus says the Lord GOD, "The city which goes forth a thousand *strong* Will have a hundred left, And the one which goes forth a hundred *strong* Will have ten left to the house of Israel."

    C' ⁴ For thus says the LORD to the house of Israel, "Seek Me that you may live. ⁵ "But do not resort to Bethel And do not come to Gilgal, Nor cross over to Beersheba; For Gilgal will certainly go into captivity And Bethel will come to trouble.

    B' ⁶ "Seek the LORD that you may live, Or He will break forth like a fire, O house of Joseph, And it will consume with none to quench *it* for Bethel, ⁷ *For* those who turn justice into wormwood And cast righteousness down to the earth."

A' ⁸ He who made the Pleiades and Orion And changes deep darkness into morning, Who also darkens day *into* night, Who calls for the waters of the sea And pours them out on the surface of the earth, The LORD is His name.

A ⁹ It is He who flashes forth *with* destruction upon the strong, So that destruction comes upon the fortress. ¹⁰ They hate him who reproves in the gate, And they abhor him who speaks *with* integrity. ¹¹ Therefore because you impose heavy rent on the poor And exact a tribute of grain from them, *Though* you have built houses of well-hewn stone, Yet you will not live in them; You have planted pleasant vineyards, yet you will not drink their wine. ¹² For I know your transgressions are many and your sins are great, *You* who distress the righteous *and* accept bribes And turn aside the poor in the gate. ¹³ Therefore at such a time the prudent person keeps silent, for it is an evil time.

    B ¹⁴ Seek good and not evil, that you may live; And thus may the LORD God of hosts be with you, Just as you have said!

    B' ¹⁵ Hate evil, love good, And establish justice in the gate! Perhaps the LORD God of hosts May be gracious to the remnant of Joseph.

A' ¹⁶ Therefore thus says the LORD God of hosts, the Lord, "There is wailing in all the plazas, And in all the streets they say, 'Alas! Alas!' They also call the farmer to mourning And professional mourners to lamentation. ¹⁷ "And in all the vineyards *there is* wailing, Because I will pass through the midst of you," says the LORD.

A ¹⁸ Alas, you who are longing for the day of the LORD, For what purpose *will* the day of the LORD *be* to you? It *will be* darkness and not light; ¹⁹ As when a man flees from a lion And a bear meets him, Or goes home, leans his hand against the wall And a snake bites him, ²⁰ *Will* not the day of the LORD *be* darkness instead of light, Even gloom with no brightness in it?

    B ²¹ "I hate, I reject your festivals, Nor do I delight in your solemn assemblies. ²² "Even though you offer up to Me burnt offerings and your grain offerings, I will not accept *them*; And I will not *even* look at the peace offerings of your fatlings. [23] "Take away from Me the noise of your songs; I will not even listen to the sound of your harps.

C [24] "But let justice roll down like waters And righteousness like an ever-flowing stream.

B' [25] "Did you present Me with sacrifices and grain offerings in the wilderness for forty years, O house of Israel? [26] "You also carried along Sikkuth your king and Kiyyun, your images, the star of your gods which you made for yourselves.

A' [27] "Therefore, I will make you go into exile beyond Damascus," says the LORD, whose name is the God of hosts.

A: Sufferings. B: Offerings. C: Justice.[31]

Discussion

This chapter comprises three chiasms. The basic message is that the LORD is coming to pronounce His judgment. Perhaps there are words of hope in this chapter. If the Israelites followed the word of the LORD and the words of Amos, they would stop sinning and that might stop what the LORD was about to bring upon them.

Questioning the Passage

1. Why is Israel called a virgin? (v. 2)

   Israel was a virgin because from the day of her inception to that moment in time, no foreign king ruled over her. Israel was never invaded until the Assyrians.

2. Why are the Israelites told not to resort to Bethel or Gilgal? (v. 5)

   Bethel was the city that King Jeroboam placed a golden calf.

   [28] So the king consulted, and made two golden calves, and he said to them, "It is too much for you to go up to Jerusalem; behold your gods, O Israel, that brought you up from the land of Egypt." [29] He set one in Bethel, and the other he put in Dan. (1 Ki. 12:28-29 NAU)

   Thus, Bethel was a city of idolatry. Gilgal was known for its altars to the gods of the Canaanites.[32]

---

[31] "Literary Structure (chiasm, Chiasmus) of Book of Amos." Literary Structure (chiasm, Chiasmus) of Each Pericopes of Book of Amos. Accessed December 12, 2017.
http://www.bible.literarystructure.info/bible/30_Amos_pericope_e.html.
[32] Scherman, Nosson, Meir Zlotowitz, Sheah Brander, and Menachem Davis. "Amos." In *The Prophets: The Later Prophets with a Commentary Anthologized from the Rabbinic Writings*. Brooklyn, NY: Mesorah Publications, 2013.

3. Why is the house of Joseph referred to in verse 6?

   The Sage Malbim[33] interprets this verse as a reference to the split in the Northern Kingdom caused by the opposition of Hosea ben Elah, the last king of Israel. Israel was involved in its own civil war.[34]

4. What is wormwood? (v. 7)

   Wormwood is a shrub with a bitter, aromatic taste. It is metaphorically used here to tell the people of the Northern Kingdom that the LORD was angry with them because the rich oppressed the poor by a corruption of the justice system. The judges were supposed to bring righteousness to the land by defending all people, especially the poor. Since the judges of the Northern Kingdom were not stopping the oppression of the poor, the LORD added this offense to the ones already on His list.

5. What is the difference between transgressions and sins? (v. 12)

   A transgression is a breach of trust or rebellion. A breach of trust against the LORD was sinful. Therefore, all transgressions can be viewed as sins. Not all sins are transgressions. The LORD was telling the people through Amos that He knows of their rebellion against the Laws of the LORD, and He also knows about their sins.

6. What is the symbolism of "the gate"? (v. 15)

   At the gate of the cities in Amos' time, there were the judges of the city who would sit and listen to the various cases that would be brought before them. To establish justice at the gate of the city meant that impartial judges who did not look at the social or financial status of the parties involved would offer fair and true rulings based on the Torah.

---

[33] 'Malbim' is an acronym of the full name of Rabbi Meir Leibush ben Yechiel Michel. Malbim was born at Volochisk, in Volhynia Russia, in 1809. He was still a child when his father died. He was educated in Hebrew and Talmud first by his father, and then by his stepfather, R. Löb of Volochisk. He studied in his native town until he was thirteen. He showed unusual talent from his early childhood. His works indicate that he also had a considerable knowledge of secular sciences. Source: http://www.malbim.org/ (The Malbim n.d.)

[34] IBID.

7. What is the symbolism of verse 19?

When a man flees from one problem, another problem arises and taunts him. It does not matter how much he runs, trouble will find him. The Israelites are being told if they try to run away from the justice of the LORD, that the LORD will pursue them until the LORD's justice is executed.[35]

8. What is the symbolism of verse 24?

Amos tells the Israelites that they must let justice be seen and executed on the land.[36]

9. What is the reference in verse 25?

This is a reference to the forty years the Israelites walked in the desert of Sinai until the LORD determined they were ready to move into the Promised Land.

10. Who were Sikkuth and Kiyyun? (v. 26)

"The prophet Amos seems to mention Sikkuth with Kiyyun, and both these names are eerily reminiscent of the names of a known Babylonian and Assyrian deity, namely Sak-kut a.k.a. Kaiwanu (a.k.a. Ninib). These names both appear to refer to Saturn, and were showed to be associated in the Shurpu tablets (says the venerable William Rainy Harper on page 140 of his opus *A Critical and Exegetical Commentary on Amos and Hosea* and leaves the following handy reference for easy verification: IV. R. 52, col. 4, l. 9).

A problem with this is that Amos speaks of the doings of the Israelites during the wandering years, and in the time just after the Exodus, Babylonian and Assyrian deities were not yet introduced in the area where Israel wandered, nor is such idolatry mentioned anywhere in the Torah (according to 2 Kings 17:30, the various Babylonian deities were introduced in Canaan by Babylonian settlers immediately after the second deportation in about 720 BC)."[37]

---

[35] IBID.

[36] IBID.

[37] Publications, Arie Uittenbogaard for Abarim. "The Amazing Name Sikkuth: Meaning and Etymology." Abarim Publications. Accessed December 12, 2017. http://www.abarim-publications.com/Meaning/Sikkuth.html#.WjAx-UqnH-g.

Main/Center Point

This chapter is a lament over the sins of Israel, the Northern Kingdom. The main sins appear to be oppressing the poor and the worship of false gods. The idea of the Day of the LORD is introduced. It will be a dark day when the LORD returns. The people may try to appease the LORD with their sacrifices and burned offerings which the LORD will reject. The peoples' sins have become too great for the LORD to forgive them without punishment.

People's names

1. סִכּוּת *Sikkuth* **Meaning:** a heathen god

2. כִּיּוּן *Kiyyun* **Meaning:** a heathen god

Name of places

1. בֵּיתְאֵל *Betheel* **Meaning:** 'house of God,' a city in Ephraim

2. גִּלְגָּל *Gilgal* **Meaning:** 'circle (of stones),' the name of several places in Palestine

3. בְּאֵר שֶׁבַע *Beer Sheba* **Meaning:** 'well of seven,' a place in the Negev

4. כִּימָה *Kimah* **Meaning:** *a cluster of stars* - Pleiades

5. כְּסִיל *Kesil* **Meaning:** a heavenly constellation - Orion

6. דַּמֶּשֶׂק *Dammeseq* **Meaning:** a city in Aram (Syria)

Scripture cross references

Verse 2	Jer 14:17; Isa 51:18; Jer 50:32
Verse 3	Isa 6:13
Verse 18	Isa 5:19; Jer 30:7; Joe 1:15; Joe 2:1, Joe 2:11, 31; Isa 5:30; Joe 2:2
Verse 19	Job 20:24; Isa 24:17, Isa 24:18; Jer 15:2, Jer 15:3; Jer 48:44
Verse 26	Act 7:43

Cultural Section

Questioning the passage

1. What were professional mourners? (v. 16)

    There was a profession for mourners who would be called by a family to help people at the funeral and later at the home of the deceased to weep over the dead.[38]

Thoughts

The wealthy people of the Northern Kingdom were exploiting and oppressing the poor people of the Kingdom. They did this by controlling the justice system. When money or politics enter the justice system of any society, then true justice most likely will not be rendered. Politics has moved into the justice system in the United States. Judges are being selected based on their political slant rather than their knowledge of the law. Even in the church, this is happening. The court system of the church, no matter what denomination it is, must be composed of people who will listen to situations and render justice based on the Laws of the LORD and the rules of the church. In many cased today, politics has entered the church courts and justice is being rendered by social activists rather than on the Law of the LORD.

---

[38] Errico, Rocco A., and George M. Lamsa. "Amos." In *Aramaic Light on Ezekiel, Daniel, and the Minor Prophets: A Commentary Based on the Aramaic Language and Ancient Near Eastern Customs*. Smyma, GA: Noohra Foundation, 2012.

Amos Chapter 6

Language

New American Standard 1995	Hebrew

<table>
<tr><td>

¹ Alas for those who are at ease in Zion, and for those who feel secure on Mount Samaria, the notables of the first of the nations, to whom the house of Israel resorts!

² Cross over to Calneh, and see; from there go to Hamath the great; then go down to Gath of the Philistines. Are you better than these kingdoms? Or is your territory greater than their territory,

³ O you that put far away the evil day, and bring near a reign of violence?

⁴ Alas for those who lie on beds of ivory, and lounge on their couches, and eat lambs from the flock, and calves from the stall;

⁵ who sing idle songs to the sound of the harp, and like David improvise on instruments of music;

⁶ who drink wine from bowls, and anoint themselves with the finest oils, but are not grieved over the ruin of Joseph!

⁷ Therefore they shall now be the first to go into exile, and the revelry of the loungers shall pass away.

⁸ The Lord GOD has sworn by himself (says the LORD, the God of hosts): I abhor the pride of Jacob and hate his strongholds; and I will deliver up the city and all that is in it.

⁹ If ten people remain in one house, they shall die.

¹⁰ And if a relative, one who burns the dead, shall take up the body to bring it out of the house, and shall say to someone in the innermost parts of the house, "Is anyone else with you?" the answer will come, "No." Then the relative shall say, "Hush! We must not mention the name of the LORD."

¹¹ See, the LORD commands, and the great house shall be shattered to bits, and the little house to pieces.

¹² Do horses run on rocks? Does one plow the sea with oxen? But you have turned justice into poison and the fruit of righteousness into wormwood--

¹³ you who rejoice in Lo-debar, who say, "Have we not by our own strength taken Karnaim for ourselves?"

¹⁴ Indeed, I am raising up against you a nation, O house of Israel, says the LORD, the God of hosts, and they shall oppress you from Lebo-hamath to the Wadi Arabah.

</td><td dir="rtl">

הֹ֣וי הַשַּׁאֲנַנִּ֣ים בְּצִיֹּ֗ון וְהַבֹּטְחִ֖ים בְּהַ֣ר שֹׁמְרֹ֑ון נְקֻבֵי֙ רֵאשִׁ֣ית הַגֹּויִ֔ם וּבָ֥אוּ לָהֶ֖ם בֵּ֥ית יִשְׂרָאֵֽל׃

² עִבְר֤וּ כַֽלְנֵה֙ וּרְא֔וּ וּלְכ֥וּ מִשָּׁ֖ם חֲמַ֣ת רַבָּ֑ה וּרְד֣וּ גַת־פְּלִשְׁתִּ֗ים הֲטֹובִים֙ מִן־הַמַּמְלָכֹ֣ות הָאֵ֔לֶּה אִם־רַ֥ב גְּבוּלָ֖ם מִגְּבֻלְכֶֽם׃

³ הַֽמְנַדִּ֖ים לְיֹ֣ום רָ֑ע וַתַּגִּישׁ֖וּן שֶׁ֥בֶת חָמָֽס׃

⁴ הַשֹּׁכְבִים֙ עַל־מִטֹּ֣ות שֵׁ֔ן וּסְרֻחִ֖ים עַל־עַרְשֹׂותָ֑ם וְאֹכְלִ֤ים כָּרִים֙ מִצֹּ֔אן וַעֲגָלִ֖ים מִתֹּ֥וךְ מַרְבֵּֽק׃

⁵ הַפֹּרְטִ֖ים עַל־פִּ֣י הַנָּ֑בֶל כְּדָוִ֕יד חָשְׁב֥וּ לָהֶ֖ם כְּלֵי־שִֽׁיר׃

⁶ הַשֹּׁתִ֤ים בְּמִזְרְקֵי֙ יַ֔יִן וְרֵאשִׁ֥ית שְׁמָנִ֖ים יִמְשָׁ֑חוּ וְלֹ֥א נֶחְל֖וּ עַל־שֵׁ֥בֶר יֹוסֵֽף׃

⁷ לָכֵ֛ן עַתָּ֥ה יִגְל֖וּ בְּרֹ֣אשׁ גֹּלִ֑ים וְסָ֖ר מִרְזַ֥ח סְרוּחִֽים׃ פ

⁸ נִשְׁבַּע֩ אֲדֹנָ֨י יְהוִ֜ה בְּנַפְשֹׁ֗ו נְאֻם־יְהוָה֙ אֱלֹהֵ֣י צְבָאֹ֔ות מְתָאֵ֤ב אָֽנֹכִי֙ אֶת־גְּאֹ֣ון יַֽעֲקֹ֔ב וְאַרְמְנֹתָ֖יו שָׂנֵ֑אתִי וְהִסְגַּרְתִּ֖י עִ֥יר וּמְלֹאָֽהּ׃

⁹ וְהָיָ֗ה אִם־יִוָּֽתְר֞וּ עֲשָׂרָ֧ה אֲנָשִׁ֛ים בְּבַ֥יִת אֶחָ֖ד וָמֵֽתוּ׃

¹⁰ וּנְשָׂאֹ֞ו דֹּודֹ֣ו וּמְסָרְפֹ֗ו לְהֹוצִ֣יא עֲצָמִים֮ מִן־הַבַּיִת֒ וְאָמַ֞ר לַאֲשֶׁ֨ר בְּיַרְכְּתֵ֤י הַבַּ֨יִת֙ הַעֹ֣וד עִמָּ֔ךְ וְאָמַ֖ר אָ֑פֶס וְאָמַ֣ר הָ֔ס כִּ֛י לֹ֥א לְהַזְכִּ֖יר בְּשֵׁ֥ם יְהוָֽה׃

¹¹ כִּֽי־הִנֵּ֤ה יְהוָה֙ מְצַוֶּ֔ה וְהִכָּ֛ה הַבַּ֥יִת הַגָּדֹ֖ול רְסִיסִ֑ים וְהַבַּ֥יִת הַקָּטֹ֖ן בְּקִעִֽים׃

¹² הַיְרֻצ֤וּן בַּסֶּ֨לַע֙ סוּסִ֔ים אִֽם־יַחֲרֹ֖ושׁ בַּבְּקָרִ֑ים כִּֽי־הֲפַכְתֶּ֤ם לְרֹאשׁ֙ מִשְׁפָּ֔ט וּפְרִ֥י צְדָקָ֖ה לְלַעֲנָֽה׃

¹³ הַשְּׂמֵחִ֖ים לְלֹ֣א דָבָ֑ר הָאֹ֣מְרִ֔ים הֲלֹ֣וא בְחָזְקֵ֔נוּ לָקַ֥חְנוּ לָ֖נוּ קַרְנָֽיִם׃

</td></tr>
</table>

<table>
<tr><td></td><td dir="rtl">14 כִּֽי הִנְנֵ֣י מֵקִ֣ים עֲלֵיכֶ֡ם בֵּית֩ יִשְׂרָאֵ֨ל נְאֻם־
יְהֹוָ֜ה אֱלֹהֵ֤י הַצְּבָאוֹת֙ גּ֔וֹי וְלָחֲצ֣וּ אֶתְכֶ֗ם
מִלְּב֥וֹא חֲמָ֖ת עַד־נַ֥חַל הָעֲרָבָֽה׃ ס</td></tr>
</table>

Process of Discovery

Linguistics Section

Linguistic Structure

A [1] Alas for those who are at ease in Zion, and for those who feel secure on Mount Samaria, the notables of the first of the nations, to whom the house of Israel resorts! [2] Cross over to Calneh, and see; from there go to Hamath the great; then go down to Gath of the Philistines. Are you better than these kingdoms? Or is your territory greater than their territory,

>**B** [3] O you that put far away the evil day, and bring near a reign of violence? [4] Alas for those who lie on beds of ivory, and lounge on their couches, and eat lambs from the flock, and calves from the stall; [5] who sing idle songs to the sound of the harp, and like David improvise on instruments of music; [6] who drink wine from bowls, and anoint themselves with the finest oils, but are not grieved over the ruin of Joseph! [7] Therefore they shall now be the first to go into exile, and the revelry of the loungers shall pass away.

>>**C** [8] The Lord GOD has sworn by himself (says the LORD, the God of hosts): I abhor the pride of Jacob and hate his strongholds; and I will deliver up the city and all that is in it. [9] If ten people remain in one house, they shall die. [10] And if a relative, one who burns the dead, shall take up the body to bring it out of the house, and shall say to someone in the innermost parts of the house, "Is anyone else with you?" the answer will come, "No." Then the relative shall say, "Hush! We must not mention the name of the LORD. [11] See, the LORD commands, and the great house shall be shattered to bits, and the little house to pieces.

>**B'** [12] Do horses run on rocks? Does one plow the sea with oxen? But you have turned justice into poison and the fruit of righteousness into wormwood--

A' [13] you who rejoice in Lo-debar, who say, "Have we not by our own strength taken Karnaim for ourselves?" [14] Indeed, I am raising up against you a nation, O house of Israel, says the LORD, the God of hosts, and they shall oppress you from Lebo-hamath to the Wadi Arabah.

Discussion

This chapter is an A-B-C chiasm. Several of the blocks comprise several verses.

Questioning the Passage

1. Where was Calneh located? (v. 2)

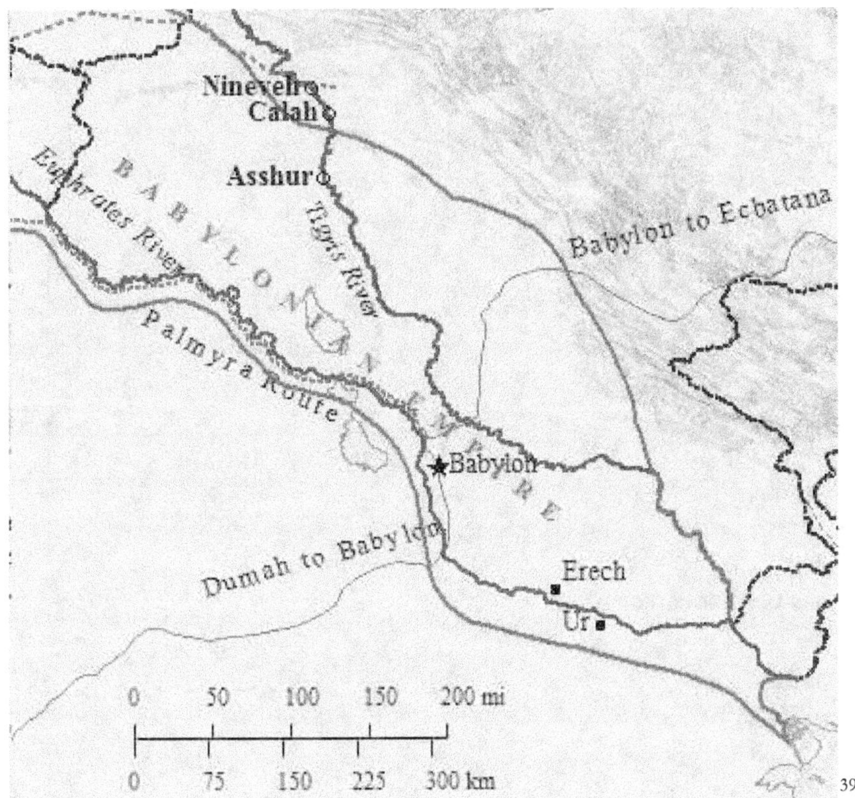

[39] "The History of Israel." Israel-a-history-of.com. Accessed December 13, 2017. http://www.israel-a-history-of.com/.

2. Where was Hamath the great located? (v. 2)

3. Where was Gath located? (v. 2)

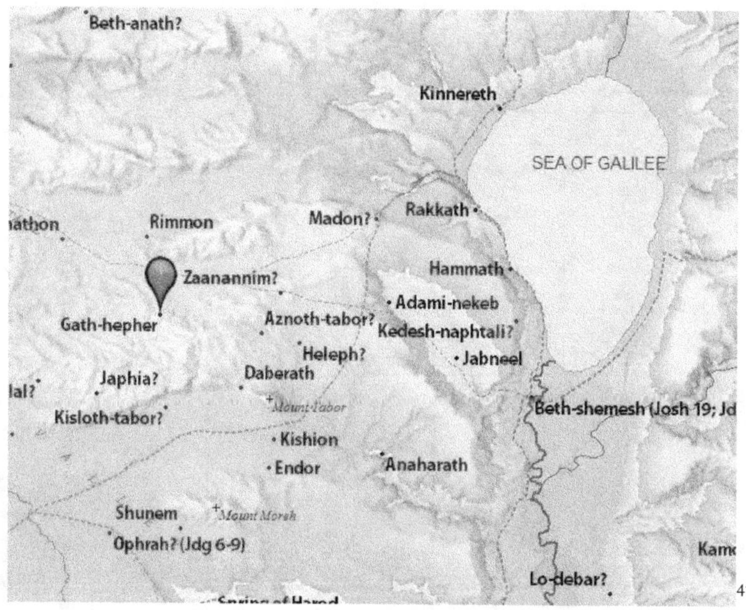

4. What was the day of calamity? (v. 3)

The Targum refers to the day of evil. The people were hearing the prophets of the LORD but had decided that the day of evil, which is equivalent to the Day of the LORD, was in the distant future. Therefore, they did not have to worry or change their ways.

---

[40] "Hama." Wikipedia. December 11, 2017. Accessed December 13, 2017. (Hamath n.d.).

[41] "Jonah Was From Gath Hepher." Leon's Message Board. October 05, 2011. Accessed December 13, 2017. https://bleon1.wordpress.com/2011/10/05/jonah-was-from-gath-hepher/.

5. What was the seat of violence? (v. 3)

The seat of violence is a reference to the unethical decision of the judges who assisted the rich to oppress the poor by ruling against the poor.

6. Who are the people described in verses 4 through 6?

The people described in these verses are the rich people of Israel. They continued their lives of luxury on the backs of the rest of the people of the nation.

7. What was the sprawlers' banquet? (v. 7)

The banquets that the rich people held for themselves would end when the LORD passed judgment upon the people. The LORD sent the Assyrian army to punish the people of the Northern Kingdom because of their exploitation of the poor.

8. Where was Lodebar? (v. 13)

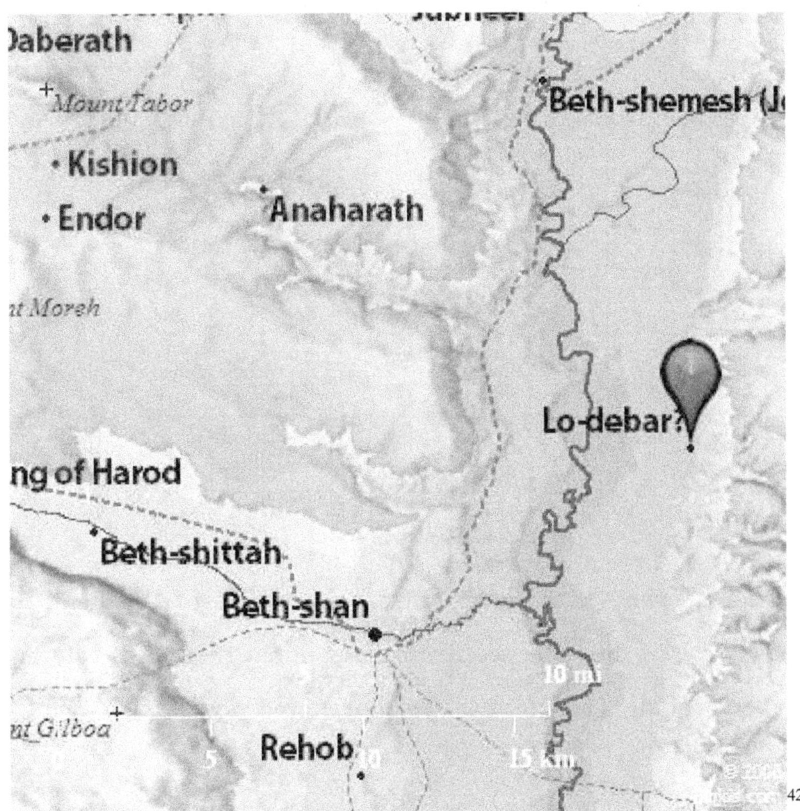

---

42 Bible Map: Lo-debar. Accessed December 13, 2017. http://bibleatlas.org/lo-debar.htm.

9. Where was the brook of the Arabah? (v. 14)

[43]

Main/Center Point

This chapter discusses the self-indulgence of the rich people of Israel and Judah. The rich people were taking advantage of the poor people of the country. Instead of offering charity to the poor, they did what they could to ensure that the poor stayed poor, thus serving the rich. The LORD

---

[43] Bible-archeology-exodus-kadesh-barnea-arabah. Accessed December 13, 2017. (The Arabah, The way of Arabah, Arabah Road n.d.).

considered this an indulgence that needed to be repented, if not, the LORD was going to punish the rich by having their riches, i.e. homes, destroyed by an invading army.

People's names

1. דָּוִד *David* or דָּוִיד *David* **Meaning:** perhaps 'beloved one,' a son of Jesse
2. יַעֲקֹב *Yaaqob* **Meaning:** a son of Isaac, also his descendants

Name of places

1. צִיּוֹן *Tsiyyon* **Meaning:** a mountain in Israel, also a name for Jerusalem
2. שֹׁמְרוֹן *Shomron* **Meaning:** capital of Northern kingdom of Israel
3. כַּלְנֵה *Kalneh* **Meaning:** a city conquered by Assyria
4. חֲמָת *Chamath* **Meaning:** a place north of Damascus
5. גַּת *Gath* **Meaning:** 'wine press,' a Philistine city
6. חֲמָת *Chamath* **Meaning:** a place north of Damascus
7. עֲרָבָה *arabah* **Meaning:** *a steppe* or *desert plain,* also a desert valley running south from the Sea of Galilee

Scripture cross references

Verse 1   Isa 32:9-11; Zep 1:12; Luk 6:24; Exo 19:5

Verse 4   Eze 34:2, Eze 34:3

Verse 5   1Ch 15:16; 1Ch 23:5; Isa 5:12

Verse 14   Jer 5:15; Num 34:7, Num 34:8; 1Ki 8:65; 2Ki 14:25

Thoughts

In Amos' time, the rich people had forgotten that their wealth was generated by the work of the poor people of the nation. They should have been generous to the poor since they had so much. The LORD expects that people who know how to make money will share their excess with others. A problem at that time was that in the Northern Kingdom the rich were continuing to exploit the poor even though they were rich. How much money and property does one need? If you asked the richest person on the planet today, they would probably say that they did not have enough wealth.

Is there not a point where one has more than one needs? How does one determine how much is enough? If you are not exploiting others to acquire your wealth, then you have nothing to be concerned about.

Amos Chapter 7

Language

New American Standard 1995	Hebrew
[1] Thus the Lord GOD showed me, and behold, He was forming a locust-swarm when the spring crop began to sprout. And behold, the spring crop *was* after the king's mowing. [2] And it came about, when it had finished eating the vegetation of the land, that I said, "Lord GOD, please pardon! How can Jacob stand, For he is small?" [3] The LORD changed His mind about this. "It shall not be," said the LORD. [4] Thus the Lord GOD showed me, and behold, the Lord GOD was calling to contend *with them* by fire, and it consumed the great deep and began to consume the farm land. [5] Then I said, "Lord GOD, please stop! How can Jacob stand, for he is small?" [6] The LORD changed His mind about this. "This too shall not be," said the Lord GOD. [7] Thus He showed me, and behold, the Lord was standing by a vertical wall with a plumb line in His hand. [8] The LORD said to me, "What do you see, Amos?" And I said, "A plumb line." Then the Lord said, "Behold I am about to put a plumb line In the midst of My people Israel. I will spare them no longer. [9] "The high places of Isaac will be desolated And the sanctuaries of Israel laid waste. Then I will rise up against the house of Jeroboam with the sword." [10] Then Amaziah, the priest of Bethel, sent *word* to Jeroboam king of Israel, saying, "Amos has conspired against you in the midst of the house of Israel; the land is unable to endure all his words. [11] "For thus Amos says, 'Jeroboam will die by the sword and Israel will certainly go from its land into exile.'" [12] Then Amaziah said to Amos, "Go, you seer, flee away to the land of Judah and there eat bread and there do your prophesying! [13] "But no longer prophesy at Bethel, for it is a sanctuary of the king and a royal residence." [14] Then Amos replied to Amaziah, "I am not a prophet, nor am I the son of a prophet; for I am a herdsman and a grower of sycamore figs.	¹ כֹּה הִרְאַנִי אֲדֹנָי יְהוִה וְהִנֵּה יוֹצֵר גֹּבַי בִּתְחִלַּת עֲלוֹת הַלָּקֶשׁ וְהִנֵּה־לֶקֶשׁ אַחַר גִּזֵּי הַמֶּלֶךְ: ² וְהָיָה אִם־כִּלָּה לֶאֱכוֹל אֶת־עֵשֶׂב הָאָרֶץ וָאֹמַר אֲדֹנָי יְהוִה סְלַח־נָא מִי יָקוּם יַעֲקֹב כִּי קָטֹן הוּא: ³ נִחַם יְהוָה עַל־זֹאת לֹא תִהְיֶה אָמַר יְהוָה: ⁴ כֹּה הִרְאַנִי אֲדֹנָי יְהוִה וְהִנֵּה קֹרֵא לָרִב בָּאֵשׁ אֲדֹנָי יְהוִה וַתֹּאכַל אֶת־תְּהוֹם רַבָּה וְאָכְלָה אֶת־הַחֵלֶק: ⁵ וָאֹמַר אֲדֹנָי יְהוִה חֲדַל־נָא מִי יָקוּם יַעֲקֹב כִּי קָטֹן הוּא: ⁶ נִחַם יְהוָה עַל־זֹאת גַּם־הִיא לֹא תִהְיֶה אָמַר אֲדֹנָי יְהוִה: ס ⁷ כֹּה הִרְאַנִי וְהִנֵּה אֲדֹנָי נִצָּב עַל־חוֹמַת אֲנָךְ וּבְיָדוֹ אֲנָךְ: ⁸ וַיֹּאמֶר יְהוָה אֵלַי מָה־אַתָּה רֹאֶה עָמוֹס וָאֹמַר אֲנָךְ וַיֹּאמֶר אֲדֹנָי הִנְנִי שָׂם אֲנָךְ בְּקֶרֶב עַמִּי יִשְׂרָאֵל לֹא־אוֹסִיף עוֹד עֲבוֹר לוֹ: ⁹ וְנָשַׁמּוּ בָּמוֹת יִשְׂחָק וּמִקְדְּשֵׁי יִשְׂרָאֵל יֶחֱרָבוּ וְקַמְתִּי עַל־בֵּית יָרָבְעָם בֶּחָרֶב: פ ¹⁰ וַיִּשְׁלַח אֲמַצְיָה כֹּהֵן בֵּית־אֵל אֶל־יָרָבְעָם מֶלֶךְ־יִשְׂרָאֵל לֵאמֹר קָשַׁר עָלֶיךָ עָמוֹס בְּקֶרֶב בֵּית יִשְׂרָאֵל לֹא־תוּכַל הָאָרֶץ לְהָכִיל אֶת־כָּל־דְּבָרָיו: ¹¹ כִּי־כֹה אָמַר עָמוֹס בַּחֶרֶב יָמוּת יָרָבְעָם וְיִשְׂרָאֵל גָּלֹה יִגְלֶה מֵעַל אַדְמָתוֹ: ס ¹² וַיֹּאמֶר אֲמַצְיָה אֶל־עָמוֹס חֹזֶה לֵךְ בְּרַח־לְךָ אֶל־אֶרֶץ יְהוּדָה וֶאֱכָל־שָׁם לֶחֶם וְשָׁם תִּנָּבֵא: ¹³ וּבֵית־אֵל לֹא־תוֹסִיף עוֹד לְהִנָּבֵא כִּי מִקְדַּשׁ־מֶלֶךְ הוּא וּבֵית מַמְלָכָה הוּא: ס

¹⁴ וַיַּעַן עָמוֹס וַיֹּאמֶר אֶל־אֲמַצְיָה לֹא־נָבִיא אָנֹכִי וְלֹא בֶן־נָבִיא אָנֹכִי כִּי־בוֹקֵר אָנֹכִי וּבוֹלֵס שִׁקְמִים:

¹⁵ וַיִּקָּחֵנִי יְהֹוָה מֵאַחֲרֵי הַצֹּאן וַיֹּאמֶר אֵלַי יְהֹוָה לֵךְ הִנָּבֵא אֶל־עַמִּי יִשְׂרָאֵל:

¹⁶ וְעַתָּה שְׁמַע דְּבַר־יְהֹוָה אַתָּה אֹמֵר לֹא תִנָּבֵא עַל־יִשְׂרָאֵל וְלֹא תַטִּיף עַל־בֵּית יִשְׂחָק:

¹⁷ לָכֵן כֹּה־אָמַר יְהֹוָה אִשְׁתְּךָ בָּעִיר תִּזְנֶה וּבָנֶיךָ וּבְנֹתֶיךָ בַּחֶרֶב יִפֹּלוּ וְאַדְמָתְךָ בַּחֶבֶל תְּחֻלָּק וְאַתָּה עַל־אֲדָמָה טְמֵאָה תָּמוּת וְיִשְׂרָאֵל גָּלֹה יִגְלֶה מֵעַל אַדְמָתוֹ: ס

¹⁵ "But the LORD took me from following the flock and the LORD said to me, 'Go prophesy to My people Israel.'

¹⁶ "Now hear the word of the LORD: you are saying, 'You shall not prophesy against Israel nor shall you speak against the house of Isaac.'

¹⁷ "Therefore, thus says the LORD, 'Your wife will become a harlot in the city, your sons and your daughters will fall by the sword, your land will be parceled up by a *measuring* line and you yourself will die upon unclean soil. Moreover, Israel will certainly go from its land into exile.'"

Process of Discovery

Linguistics Section

Linguistic Structure

A [1] Thus the Lord GOD showed me, and behold, He was forming a locust-swarm when the spring crop began to sprout. And behold, the spring crop *was* after the king's mowing.

    B [2] And it came about, when it had finished eating the vegetation of the land, that I said, "Lord GOD, please pardon! How can Jacob stand, For he is small?"

        C [3] The LORD changed His mind about this. "It shall not be," said the LORD.

A' [4] Thus the Lord GOD showed me, and behold, the Lord GOD was calling to contend *with them* by fire, and it consumed the great deep and began to consume the farm land.

    B' [5] Then I said, "Lord GOD, please stop! How can Jacob stand, for he is small?"

        C' [6] The LORD changed His mind about this. "This too shall not be," said the Lord GOD.

A [7] Thus He showed me, and behold, the Lord was standing by a vertical wall with a plumb line in His hand. [8] The LORD said to me, "What do you see, Amos?"

    B And I said, "A plumb line."

A Then the Lord said, "Behold I am about to put a plumb line In the midst of My people Israel. I will spare them no longer. [9] "The high places of Isaac will be desolated And the sanctuaries of Israel laid waste. Then I will rise up against the house of Jeroboam with the sword."

A [10] Then Amaziah, the priest of Bethel, sent *word* to Jeroboam king of Israel, saying, "Amos has conspired against you in the midst of the house of Israel; the land is unable to endure all his words. [11] "For thus Amos says, 'Jeroboam will die by the sword and Israel will certainly go from its land into exile.'"

    B [12] Then Amaziah said to Amos, "Go, you seer, flee away to the land of Judah and there eat bread and there do your prophesying! [13] "But no longer prophesy at Bethel, for it is a sanctuary of the king and a royal residence."

        C [14] Then Amos replied to Amaziah, "I am not a prophet, nor am I the son of a prophet; for I am a herdsman and a grower of sycamore figs. [15] "But the LORD took me from following the flock and the LORD said to me, 'Go prophesy to My people Israel.'

    B' [16] "Now hear the word of the LORD: you are saying, 'You shall not prophesy against Israel nor shall you speak against the house of Isaac.'

A' [17] "Therefore, thus says the LORD, 'Your wife will become a harlot in the city, your sons and your daughters will fall by the sword, your land will be parceled up by a *measuring* line and you yourself will die upon unclean soil. Moreover, Israel will certainly go from its land into exile.'"

Discussion

This chapter comprises three chiasms. In the first chiasm, Amos asks the LORD to forgive the people of Israel. In the second chiasm, the LORD tells Amos what the judgment and punishment was in store for Israel, because they violated the covenant. The punishment could not be stopped. In the third chiasm, Amos is chased out of the land of Israel. This is the typical response of the King to the words of God's prophets.

Questioning the Passage

1. What is the king's mowing? (v. 1)

    The Targum of Amos says the "king's early harvest." The locust will attack the crops after the first harvest was over.

2. What is the symbolism of the locust-swarm? (v. 1)

    The locust is a symbol of destruction and famine. When the locust devour a field, there is no way to replace the lost food. The land could grow enough food to feed the people for a season. If a drought occurred or a locust attack, the food of the field is lost for that year and a famine would occur.

3. What does "How can Jacob stand, for he is small?" mean in verse two?

    The Targum says that the question Amos was asking the LORD is how can the Israelites worship the LORD if He exiles them from the land because they would become scattered and powerless? Israel cannot worship the LORD if they are separated one from the other. Does not the LORD want worship from His Chosen People? Yes, but the people of Israel were not worshiping the LORD. They were worshiping the pagan gods of the Canaanites.

4. What is the great deep and the fire? (v. 4)

When the Israelites were in the desert, the LORD sent fire to punish them for their disobedience.[44]

> NAU **Numbers 11:1** Now the people became like those who complain of adversity in the hearing of the LORD; and when the LORD heard *it*, His anger was kindled, and the fire of the LORD burned among them and consumed *some* of the outskirts of the camp. (Num. 11:1 NAU)

The people of the Northern Kingdom were being reminded that the LORD will punish them in the Promised Land as He did in the desert of Sinai. The fire could consume the great deep, which is a sea, therefore, there would not be water for the plants and that would cause a famine in the land.

5. What does it mean that the LORD placed a plumb line amid His people? (v. 8)

The Targum says that the LORD asked Amos what he saw, and Amos responded "judgment." The plumb line is a symbol of judgment.

6. What are the high places of Isaac? (v. 9)

"The altars that the children of Isaac have built to their idols will be desolate since everyone is too preoccupied with their afflictions to worship upon them (Metzudos).

The nation is referred to here as the children of Isaac, rather than Israel, as throughout the Scripture. This is to note the contrast between Isaac himself, who allowed himself to be bound on an altar to be offered to Hashem, and his descendants, who used altars to rebel against Hashem (Radak)."[45]

7. Why is the house of Isaac mentioned in verse sixteen?

The house of Isaac is the high places of Isaac.

---

[44] Scherman, Nosson, Meir Zlotowitz, Sheah Brander, and Menachem Davis. "Amos." In *The Prophets: The Later Prophets with a Commentary Anthologized from the Rabbinic Writings*. Brooklyn, NY: Mesorah Publications, 2013.
[45] IBID.

8. What is the meaning of verse seventeen?

   This verse is referring to what was going to happen to the Northern Kingdom when the LORD sends His punishment to the people.

Main/Center Point

This chapter describes the punishment that was about to come upon the Northern Kingdom. The king was not pleased with this prophecy and told Amos to leave the country.

People's names

1. יִצְחָק *Yitschaq* **Meaning:** 'he laughs,' son of Abraham and Sarah

2. אֲמַצְיָהוּ *Amatsyahu* or אֲמַצְיָה *Amatsyah* **Meaning:** 'Yah is mighty,' the name of several Israel

3. עָמוֹס *Amos* **Meaning:** an Israel prophet

4. יָרָבְעָם *Yarobam* **Meaning:** 'the people increase,' the name of two Israelite kings

Name of places

1. בֵּיתְאֵל *Betheel* **Meaning:** 'house of God,' a city in Ephraim, also a place in south Judah

Thoughts

Creating altars to the pagan gods is pure idolatry. This is a violation of the commandment concerning idolatry. Amos relayed God's message that He had enough of the people's sin because of idolatry. Idols come today in many forms. We remember that all that we have are blessings from the LORD. We are only stewards on this earth. The LORD gives us some assets to take care of while we are here. Remember that the LORD is seeing how we use the blessings He sends us.

Amos Chapter 8 & 9

Language

New American Standard 1995	Hebrew
¹ Thus the Lord GOD showed me, and behold, *there was* a basic of summer fruit. ² He said, "What do you see, Amos?" And I said, "A basket of summer fruit." Then the LORD said to me, "The end has come for My people Israel. I will spare them no longer. ³ "The songs of the palace will turn to wailing in that day," declares the Lord GOD. "Many *will be* the corpses; in every place they will cast them forth in silence." ⁴ Hear this, you who trample the needy, to do away with the humble of the land, ⁵ saying, "When will the new moon be over, So that we may sell grain, And the sabbath, that we may open the wheat *market*, To make the bushel smaller and the shekel bigger, And to cheat with dishonest scales, ⁶ So as to buy the helpless for money And the needy for a pair of sandals, And *that* we may sell the refuse of the wheat?" ⁷ The LORD has sworn by the pride of Jacob, "Indeed, I will never forget any of their deeds. ⁸ "Because of this will not the land quake And everyone who dwells in it mourn? Indeed, all of it will rise up like the Nile, And it will be tossed about And subside like the Nile of Egypt. ⁹ "It will come about in that day," declares the Lord GOD, "That I will make the sun go down at noon And make the earth dark in broad daylight. ¹⁰ "Then I will turn your festivals into mourning And all your songs into lamentation; And I will bring sackcloth on everyone's loins And baldness on every head. And I will make it like *a time of* mourning for an only son, And the end of it will be like a bitter day. ¹¹ "Behold, days are coming," declares the Lord GOD, "When I will send a famine on the land, Not a famine for bread or a thirst for water, But rather for hearing the words of the LORD. ¹² "People will stagger from sea to sea And from the north even to the east; They will go to and fro to seek the word of the LORD, But they will not find *it*. ¹³ "In that day the beautiful virgins And the young men will faint from thirst. ¹⁴ "*As for* those who swear by the guilt of Samaria, Who say, 'As your god lives, O Dan,'	¹כֹּה הִרְאַ֫נִי אֲדֹנָ֣י יְהוִ֑ה וְהִנֵּ֖ה כְּל֣וּב קָ֑יִץ: ² וַיֹּ֗אמֶר מָֽה־אַתָּ֤ה רֹאֶה֙ עָמ֔וֹס וָאֹמַ֖ר כְּל֣וּב קָ֑יִץ וַיֹּ֤אמֶר יְהוָה֙ אֵלַ֔י בָּ֤א הַקֵּץ֙ אֶל־עַמִּ֣י יִשְׂרָאֵ֔ל לֹא־אוֹסִ֥יף ע֖וֹד עֲב֥וֹר לֽוֹ: ³ וְהֵילִ֜ילוּ שִׁיר֤וֹת הֵיכָל֙ בַּיּ֣וֹם הַה֔וּא נְאֻ֖ם אֲדֹנָ֣י יְהוִ֑ה רַ֣ב הַפֶּ֔גֶר בְּכָל־מָק֖וֹם הִשְׁלִ֥יךְ הָֽס: פ ⁴ שִׁמְעוּ־זֹ֕את הַשֹּׁאֲפִ֖ים אֶבְי֑וֹן וְלַשְׁבִּ֖ית (עֲנִוֵי־) [עֲנִיֵּי־] אָֽרֶץ: ⁵ לֵאמֹ֗ר מָתַ֞י יַעֲבֹ֤ר הַחֹ֙דֶשׁ֙ וְנַשְׁבִּ֣ירָה שֶּׁ֔בֶר וְהַשַּׁבָּ֖ת וְנִפְתְּחָה־בָּ֑ר לְהַקְטִ֤ין אֵיפָה֙ וּלְהַגְדִּ֣יל שֶׁ֔קֶל וּלְעַוֵּ֖ת מֹאזְנֵ֥י מִרְמָֽה: ⁶ לִקְנ֤וֹת בַּכֶּ֙סֶף֙ דַּלִּ֔ים וְאֶבְי֖וֹן בַּעֲב֣וּר נַעֲלָ֑יִם וּמַפַּ֥ל בַּ֖ר נַשְׁבִּֽיר: ⁷ נִשְׁבַּ֥ע יְהוָ֖ה בִּגְא֣וֹן יַעֲקֹ֑ב אִם־אֶשְׁכַּ֥ח לָנֶ֖צַח כָּל־מַעֲשֵׂיהֶֽם: ⁸ הַעַ֤ל זֹאת֙ לֹא־תִרְגַּ֣ז הָאָ֔רֶץ וְאָבַ֖ל כָּל־יוֹשֵׁ֣ב בָּ֑הּ וְעָלְתָ֤ה כָאֹר֙ כֻּלָּ֔הּ וְנִגְרְשָׁ֥ה (וְנִשְׁקָה) [וְנִשְׁקְעָה] כִּיא֖וֹר מִצְרָֽיִם: ס ⁹ וְהָיָ֣ה בַּיּ֣וֹם הַה֗וּא נְאֻם֙ אֲדֹנָ֣י יְהוִ֔ה וְהֵבֵאתִ֥י הַשֶּׁ֖מֶשׁ בַּֽצָּהֳרָ֑יִם וְהַחֲשַׁכְתִּ֥י לָאָ֖רֶץ בְּי֥וֹם אֽוֹר: ¹⁰ וְהָפַכְתִּ֨י חַגֵּיכֶ֜ם לְאֵ֗בֶל וְכָל־שִׁירֵיכֶם֙ לְקִינָ֔ה וְהַעֲלֵיתִ֤י עַל־כָּל־מָתְנַ֙יִם֙ שָׂ֔ק וְעַל־כָּל־רֹ֖אשׁ קָרְחָ֑ה וְשַׂמְתִּ֙יהָ֙ כְּאֵ֣בֶל יָחִ֔יד וְאַחֲרִיתָ֖הּ כְּי֥וֹם מָֽר: ¹¹ הִנֵּ֣ה׀ יָמִ֣ים בָּאִ֗ים נְאֻם֙ אֲדֹנָ֣י יְהוִ֔ה וְהִשְׁלַחְתִּ֥י רָעָ֖ב בָּאָ֑רֶץ לֹֽא־רָעָ֤ב לַלֶּ֙חֶם֙ וְלֹֽא־צָמָ֣א לַמַּ֔יִם כִּ֣י אִם־לִשְׁמֹ֔עַ אֵ֖ת דִּבְרֵ֥י יְהוָֽה: ¹² וְנָעוּ֙ מִיָּ֣ם עַד־יָ֔ם וּמִצָּפ֖וֹן וְעַד־מִזְרָ֑ח יְשֽׁוֹטְט֛וּ לְבַקֵּ֥שׁ אֶת־דְּבַר־יְהוָ֖ה וְלֹ֥א יִמְצָֽאוּ: ¹³ בַּיּ֣וֹם הַה֔וּא תִּתְעַלַּ֗פְנָה הַבְּתוּלֹ֥ת הַיָּפ֖וֹת וְהַבַּחוּרִ֑ים בַּצָּמָֽא:

And, 'As the way of Beersheba lives,' They will fall and not rise again."

Chapter 9:1 I saw the Lord standing beside the altar, and He said, "Smite the capitals so that the thresholds will shake, And break them on the heads of them all! Then I will slay the rest of them with the sword; They will not have a fugitive who will flee, Or a refugee who will escape.

2 "Though they dig into Sheol, From there will My hand take them; And though they ascend to heaven, From there will I bring them down.

3 "Though they hide on the summit of Carmel, I will search them out and take them from there; And though they conceal themselves from My sight on the floor of the sea, From there I will command the serpent and it will bite them.

4 "And though they go into captivity before their enemies, From there I will command the sword that it slay them, And I will set My eyes against them for evil and not for good."

5 The Lord GOD of hosts, The One who touches the land so that it melts, And all those who dwell in it mourn, And all of it rises up like the Nile And subsides like the Nile of Egypt;

6 The One who builds His upper chambers in the heavens And has founded His vaulted dome over the earth, He who calls for the waters of the sea And pours them out on the face of the earth, The LORD is His name.

7 "Are you not as the sons of Ethiopia to Me, O sons of Israel?" declares the LORD. "Have I not brought up Israel from the land of Egypt, And the Philistines from Caphtor and the Arameans from Kir?

8 "Behold, the eyes of the Lord GOD are on the sinful kingdom, And I will destroy it from the face of the earth; Nevertheless, I will not totally destroy the house of Jacob," Declares the LORD.

9 "For behold, I am commanding, And I will shake the house of Israel among all nations As *grain* is shaken in a sieve, But not a kernel will fall to the ground.

10 "All the sinners of My people will die by the sword, Those who say, 'The calamity will not overtake or confront us.'

11 "In that day I will raise up the fallen booth of David, And wall up its breaches; I will also raise up its ruins And rebuild it as in the days of old;

12 That they may possess the remnant of Edom And all the nations who are called by My name," Declares the LORD who does this.

13 "Behold, days are coming," declares the LORD, "When the plowman will overtake the reaper And the treader of grapes him who sows

הַנִּשְׁבָּעִים בְּאַשְׁמַת שֹׁמְרֹון וְאָמְרוּ חֵי 14 אֱלֹהֶיךָ דָּן וְחֵי דֶּרֶךְ בְּאֵר־שָׁבַע וְנָפְלוּ וְלֹא־ יָקוּמוּ עֹוד: ס

Chapter 9:1 רָאִיתִי אֶת־אֲדֹנָי נִצָּב עַל־ הַמִּזְבֵּחַ וַיֹּאמֶר הַךְ הַכַּפְתֹּור וְיִרְעֲשׁוּ הַסִּפִּים וּבְצַעַם בְּרֹאשׁ כֻּלָּם וְאַחֲרִיתָם בַּחֶרֶב אֶהֱרֹג לֹא־יָנוּס לָהֶם נָס וְלֹא־יִמָּלֵט לָהֶם פָּלִיט:

אִם־יַחְתְּרוּ בִשְׁאֹול מִשָּׁם יָדִי תִקָּחֵם וְאִם־ 2 יַעֲלוּ הַשָּׁמַיִם מִשָּׁם אֹורִידֵם:

וְאִם־יֵחָבְאוּ בְּרֹאשׁ הַכַּרְמֶל מִשָּׁם אֲחַפֵּשׂ 3 וּלְקַחְתִּים וְאִם־יִסָּתְרוּ מִנֶּגֶד עֵינַי בְּקַרְקַע הַיָּם מִשָּׁם אֲצַוֶּה אֶת־הַנָּחָשׁ וּנְשָׁכָם:

וְאִם־יֵלְכוּ בַשְּׁבִי לִפְנֵי אֹיְבֵיהֶם מִשָּׁם אֲצַוֶּה 4 אֶת־הַחֶרֶב וַהֲרָגָתַם וְשַׂמְתִּי עֵינִי עֲלֵיהֶם לְרָעָה וְלֹא לְטֹובָה:

וַאדֹנָי יְהוִה הַצְּבָאֹות הַנֹּוגֵעַ בָּאָרֶץ וַתָּמֹוג 5 וְאָבְלוּ כָּל־יֹושְׁבֵי בָהּ וְעָלְתָה כַיְאֹר כֻּלָּהּ וְשָׁקְעָה כִּיאֹר מִצְרָיִם:

הַבֹּונֶה בַשָּׁמַיִם (מַעֲלֹותֹו) [מַעֲלֹותָיו] 6 וַאֲגֻדָּתֹו עַל־אֶרֶץ יְסָדָהּ הַקֹּרֵא לְמֵי־הַיָּם וַיִּשְׁפְּכֵם עַל־פְּנֵי הָאָרֶץ יְהוָה שְׁמֹו:

הֲלֹוא כִבְנֵי כֻשִׁיִּים אַתֶּם לִי בְּנֵי יִשְׂרָאֵל 7 נְאֻם־יְהוָה הֲלֹוא אֶת־יִשְׂרָאֵל הֶעֱלֵיתִי מֵאֶרֶץ מִצְרַיִם וּפְלִשְׁתִּיִּים מִכַּפְתֹּור וַאֲרָם מִקִּיר:

הִנֵּה עֵינֵי אֲדֹנָי יְהוִה בַּמַּמְלָכָה הַחַטָּאָה 8 וְהִשְׁמַדְתִּי אֹתָהּ מֵעַל פְּנֵי הָאֲדָמָה אֶפֶס כִּי לֹא הַשְׁמֵיד אַשְׁמִיד אֶת־בֵּית יַעֲקֹב נְאֻם־ יְהוָה:

כִּי־הִנֵּה אָנֹכִי מְצַוֶּה וַהֲנִעֹותִי בְכָל־הַגֹּויִם 9 אֶת־בֵּית יִשְׂרָאֵל כַּאֲשֶׁר יִנֹּועַ בַּכְּבָרָה וְלֹא־ יִפֹּול צְרֹור אָרֶץ:

בַּחֶרֶב יָמוּתוּ כֹּל חַטָּאֵי עַמִּי הָאֹמְרִים לֹא־ 10 תַגִּישׁ וְתַקְדִּים בַּעֲדֵינוּ הָרָעָה:

בַּיֹּום הַהוּא אָקִים אֶת־סֻכַּת דָּוִיד הַנֹּפֶלֶת 11 וְגָדַרְתִּי אֶת־פִּרְצֵיהֶן וַהֲרִסֹתָיו אָקִים וּבְנִיתִיהָ כִּימֵי עֹולָם:

לְמַעַן יִירְשׁוּ אֶת־שְׁאֵרִית אֱדֹום וְכָל־הַגֹּויִם 12 אֲשֶׁר־נִקְרָא שְׁמִי עֲלֵיהֶם נְאֻם־יְהוָה עֹשֶׂה זֹּאת: פ

<table>
<tr>
<td>

seed; When the mountains will drip sweet wine And all the hills will be dissolved.

14 "Also I will restore the captivity of My people Israel, And they will rebuild the ruined cities and live *in them*; They will also plant vineyards and drink their wine, And make gardens and eat their fruit.

15 "I will also plant them on their land, And they will not again be rooted out from their land Which I have given them," Says the LORD your God.

</td>
<td dir="rtl">

13 הִנֵּ֨ה יָמִ֤ים בָּאִים֙ נְאֻם־יְהוָ֔ה וְנִגַּ֤שׁ חוֹרֵשׁ֙ בַּקֹּצֵ֔ר וְדֹרֵ֥ךְ עֲנָבִ֖ים בְּמֹשֵׁ֣ךְ הַזָּ֑רַע וְהִטִּ֤יפוּ הֶֽהָרִים֙ עָסִ֔יס וְכָל־הַגְּבָע֖וֹת תִּתְמוֹגַֽגְנָה׃

14 וְשַׁבְתִּי֙ אֶת־שְׁב֣וּת עַמִּ֣י יִשְׂרָאֵ֔ל וּבָנ֥וּ עָרִ֛ים נְשַׁמּ֖וֹת וְיָשָׁ֑בוּ וְנָטְע֣וּ כְרָמִ֗ים וְשָׁת֖וּ אֶת־יֵינָ֑ם וְעָשׂ֣וּ גַנּ֔וֹת וְאָכְל֖וּ אֶת־פְּרִיהֶֽם׃

15 וּנְטַעְתִּ֖ים עַל־אַדְמָתָ֑ם וְלֹ֨א יִנָּתְשׁ֜וּ ע֗וֹד מֵעַ֤ל אַדְמָתָם֙ אֲשֶׁ֣ר נָתַ֣תִּי לָהֶ֔ם אָמַ֖ר יְהוָ֥ה אֱלֹהֶֽיךָ׃

</td>
</tr>
</table>

Process of Discovery

Linguistics Section

Linguistic Structure

A [1] Thus the Lord GOD showed me, and behold, *there was* a basket of summer fruit. [2] He said, "What do you see, Amos?"

    B And I said, "A basket of summer fruit."

A' Then the LORD said to me, "The end has come for My people Israel. I will spare them no longer. [3] "The songs of the palace will turn to wailing in that day," declares the Lord GOD. "Many *will be* the corpses; in every place they will cast them forth in silence."

A [4] Hear this, you who trample the needy, to do away with the humble of the land, [5] saying, "When will the new moon be over, So that we may sell grain, And the sabbath, that we may open the wheat *market*, To make the bushel smaller and the shekel bigger, And to cheat with dishonest scales, [6] So as to buy the helpless for money And the needy for a pair of sandals, And *that* we may sell the refuse of the wheat?" [7] The LORD has sworn by the pride of Jacob, "Indeed, I will never forget any of their deeds.

    B [8] "Because of this will not the land quake And everyone who dwells in it mourn? Indeed, all of it will rise up like the Nile, And it will be tossed about And subside like the Nile of Egypt.

        C [9] "It will come about in that day," declares the Lord GOD, "That I will make the sun go down at noon And make the earth dark in broad daylight. [10] "Then I will turn your festivals into mourning And all your songs into lamentation; And I will bring sackcloth on everyone's loins And baldness on every head. And I will make it like *a time of* mourning for an only son, And the end of it will be like a bitter day. [11] "Behold, days are coming," declares the Lord GOD, "When I will send a famine on the land, Not a famine for bread or a thirst for water, But rather for hearing the words of the LORD. [12] "People will stagger from sea to sea And from the north even to the east; They will go to and fro to seek the word of the LORD, But they will not find *it*.

            D [13] "In that day the beautiful virgins And the young men will faint from thirst. [14] "*As for* those who swear by the guilt of Samaria, Who say, 'As your god lives,

        C' Chapter 9:1 O Dan,' And, 'As the way of Beersheba lives,' They will fall and not rise again." I saw the Lord standing beside the altar, and He said, "Smite the capitals so that the thresholds will shake, And break them on the heads of them all! Then I will slay the rest of them with the sword; They will not have a fugitive who will flee, Or a refugee who will escape. [2] "Though they dig into Sheol, From there will My hand take them; And though they ascend to heaven, From there will I bring them down. [3] "Though they hide on the summit of Carmel, I will search them out and take them from there; And though they conceal themselves from My sight on the floor of the sea, From there I will command the serpent and it will bite them. [4] "And though they go into captivity before their enemies, From there I will command the sword that it slay them, And I will set My eyes against them for evil and not for good."

B' [5] The Lord GOD of hosts, The One who touches the land so that it melts, And all those who dwell in it mourn, And all of it rises up like the Nile And subsides like the Nile of Egypt; [6] The One who builds His upper chambers in the heavens And has founded His vaulted dome over the earth, He who calls for the waters of the sea And pours them out on the face of the earth, The LORD is His name.

A' [7] "Are you not as the sons of Ethiopia to Me, O sons of Israel?" declares the LORD. "Have I not brought up Israel from the land of Egypt, And the Philistines from Caphtor and the Arameans from Kir? [8] "Behold, the eyes of the Lord GOD are on the sinful kingdom, And I will destroy it from the face of the earth; Nevertheless, I will not totally destroy the house of Jacob," Declares the LORD. [9] "For behold, I am commanding, And I will shake the house of Israel among all nations As *grain* is shaken in a sieve, But not a kernel will fall to the ground. [10] "All the sinners of My people will die by the sword, Those who say, 'The calamity will not overtake or confront us.'

A [11] "In that day I will raise up the fallen booth of David, And wall up its breaches; I will also raise up its ruins And rebuild it as in the days of old;

> **B** [12] That they may possess the remnant of Edom And all the nations who are called by My name," Declares the LORD who does this.

A' [13] "Behold, days are coming," declares the LORD, "When the plowman will overtake the reaper And the treader of grapes him who sows seed; When the mountains will drip sweet wine And all the hills will be dissolved. [14] "Also I will restore the captivity of My people Israel, And they will rebuild the ruined cities and live *in them*; They will also plant vineyards and drink their wine, And make gardens and eat their fruit.

> **B'** [15] "I will also plant them on their land, And they will not again be rooted out from their land Which I have given them," Says the LORD your God.

Discussion

Chapters eight and nine are combined because the second chiasm starts in chapter eight and extends to chapter nine. Through Amos, the LORD repeats what He is going to do about the Northern Kingdom because of their sins and wickedness. In the final chiasm of the book, the LORD gives the people of the Northern Kingdom the hope that a remnant of the people will be restored. The people of the Northern Kingdom were destroyed. However, the Northern Kingdom was destroyed without survivors, so a question is, how will the righteous people be restored?

Questioning the Passage

1. What is the symbolism of the basket of summer fruit? (v. 8:1)

    Figs grow through the summer. These are the summer fruits.[46]

2. What is the significance of the new moon being over? (v. 8:5)

    The new moon determines the start of each month of the calendar.

3. What are the deeds described in verses 8:4 to 8:7?

    These are the calamities the LORD was to bring upon the people because of their wickedness.

4. What is the pride of Jacob? (v. 8:7)

    The Targum reads the "greatness of Jacob." The greatness of Jacob is that the LORD gave to His Chosen People His name through Moses at Sinai.

5. What is the symbolism of the Nile? (v. 8:9)

    "This alludes to the death of Josiah king of Judah at the hands of Pharaoh-Neco of Egypt, which occurred at a time when there were no hostilities between the two nations."[47]

6. What does it mean that virgins and young men will faint from thirst? (v. 8:13)

    The Targum reads that the beautiful young women of the land will become so tired from fornication that they will faint as if they were thirsty.

7. What is the reference to the sons of Ethiopia? (v. 9:7)

    The Israelites and the people of Ethiopia are descendants of Noah. The LORD is saying that if He can punish Ethiopia for their sins, he certainly can punish Israel.[48]

---

[46] IBID.

[47] IBID.

[48] IBID.

Main/Center Point

These two chapters tell of the destruction of the Northern Kingdom of Israel. As with all prophets there is a section of hope that the LORD would restore a remnant of His people. The remnant would come from the Southern Kingdom.

People's names

1. עָמוֹס *Amos* **Meaning:** an Israel prophet

Name of places

1. מִצְרָיִם *Mitsrayim* **Meaning:** a son of Ham, also his descendants and their country in north western Africa
2. בְּאֵר שֶׁבַע *Beer Sheba* **Meaning:** 'well of seven,' a place in the Negev
3. כּוּשִׁי *Kushi* **Meaning:** descendants of Cush
4. פְּלִשְׁתִּי *Pelishti* **Meaning:** inhabitants of Philistia
5. כַּפְתֹּר *Kaphtor* or כַּפְתּוֹר *Kaphtor* **Meaning:** probably a name for Crete
6. דָּוִד *David* or דָּוִיד *David* **Meaning:** perhaps. 'beloved one,' a son of Jessie, King of Israel

Scripture cross references

Verse 8:2   Jer 24:3; Eze 7:2, Eze 7:3, 6

Verse 8:9   Job 5:14; Isa 13:10; Jer 15:9; Mic 3:6; Isa 59:9, Isa 59:10;

Verse 8:10   Job 20:23; Isa 15:2, Isa 15:3; Jer 48:37; Eze 7:18; Eze 27:31; Jer 6:26; Zec 12:10

Verse 9:1   Zep 2:14; Psa 68:21; Hab 3:13; Jer 11:11

Verse 9:5   Psa 104:32; Psa 144:5; Isa 64:1; Mic 1:4

Verse 9:6   2Ch 14:9, 2Ch 14:12; Isa 20:4; Isa 43:3; Deu 2:23; Jer 47:4; 2Ki 16:9; Isa 22:6

Verse 9:10   Isa 33:14; Zec 13:8

Verse 9:14   Psa 53:6; Isa 60:4; Jer 30:3, Jer 30:18; Isa 61:4; Isa 65:21; Jer 24:6; Jer 31:28

Verse 9:15   Isa 60:21; Eze 34:28; Eze 37:25

Thoughts

The LORD sends His warning about the people's behavior through Amos. If they had cleaned up their actions, the LORD would have forgiven them. However, they did not change their ways, so the LORD had to bring the punishment. But with punishment is the hope of restoration.

Bibliography

n.d. *Amos chiasms.* Accessed December 12, 2017.

> http://www.bible.literarystructure.info/bible/30_Amos_pericope_e.html.

Austin, Steve A. n.d. *The Scientific and Scriptural Impact of Amos' Earthquake.* Accessed December 4,

> 2017. http://www.icr.org/article/scientific-scriptural-impact-amos-earthquake.

n.d. *Bashan.* Accessed December 11, 2017. http://biblehub.com/commentaries/amos/4-1.htm.

n.d. *Beth-Eden, Damascus.* Accessed December 05, 2017. http://bibleatlas.org/beth-eden.htm.

n.d. *Books of the Bible Maps.* Accessed December 04, 2017. http://www.bible-

> history.com/maps/books.php.

n.d. *Discover the meanings of thousands of Biblical names in Abarim Publications' Biblical Name Vault: Sikkuth.*

> Accessed December 12, 2017. http://www.abarim-

> publications.com/Meaning/Sikkuth.html#.WjAx-UqnH-g.

Errico, Rocco & George Lamsa. 2012. *Aramaic Light on Ezekiel, Daniel, and the Minor Prophets.* Smyma,

> GA: Noohra Foundation.

n.d. *Hamath.* Accessed December 13, 2017. https://en.wikipedia.org/wiki/Hama.

n.d. *Horvat Kerioth.* Accessed December 8, 2017. http://www.biblewalks.com/Sites/Kerioth.html.

n.d. *Kir.* Accessed December 05, 2017. http://bibleatlas.org/full/kir-hareseth.htm.

n.d. *Lodebar.* Accessed December 13, 2017. http://bibleatlas.org/lo-debar.htm.

n.d. *Map of Tekoa.* Accessed December 4, 2017. http://bibleatlas.org/tekoa.htm.

n.d. *Map of the Southern Tribes.* Accessed December 8, 2017. http://www.israel-a-history-

> of.com/map-of-palestine.html.

n.d. *Rabbi David Kimchi - RaDaK.* Accessed January 16, 2018.

> http://www.chabad.org/library/article_cdo/aid/111880/jewish/Rabbi-David-Kimchi-

> RaDaK.htm.

n.d. *Rashi.* Accessed January 16, 2018. https://www.myjewishlearning.com/article/who-was-rashi/.

n.d. *The Arabah, The way of Arabah, Arabah Road.* Accessed December 13, 2017.

> http://www.bible.ca/archeology/bible-archeology-exodus-kadesh-barnea-arabah.htm.

n.d. *The History of Israel.* Accessed December 13, 2017. http://www.israel-a-history-of.com.

n.d. *The Malbim .* Accessed January 16, 2018. http://www.malbim.org/.

n.d. *Valley of Aven.* Accessed December 05, 2017. http://bibleatlas.org/valley_of_aven.htm.

Wilson, Ralph. n.d. *Life of David.* Accessed December 05, 2017.
   http://www.jesuswalk.com/david/life_of_david_maps_and_graphics.htm.